ALEC ... THANK

DONE AND MEANT

ARE A GREAT FRIEND AND TRUE

VISIONARY.

ALL THE BEST TO

YOU AND YOUR FAMILY

Are you prosperous? Are you having the time of your life? Do you want to? Do you really know what happens behind your eyes? Would you like to learn how to get twice the results in half the time while having twice the fun? Are you ready to have the most incredible years of your life? If so, I will show you not only how to create a new vision for yourself, but also how to make vision statements work for you in your life, so that you can ultimately experience what you have always wanted: a happier, more fulfilled you, a more fulfilled, more prosperous LIFE.

GET A VISION AND LIVE IT

BECOMING PROSPEROUS NOW FOR LIFE

LARRY OLSEN

Email all inquiries to: success@aperneo.com

www.aperneo.com

Library of Congress Control Number: 2008930813

ISBN: 978-1-890427-65-8

Production Coordinator: Diane Monzelowsky
Editor: Mary Holden
Cover Design: Summit Media
Typesetting: Proof Plus

Printed in the United States of America

First Edition

1 2 3 4 5 6 7 8 9 10

Although the author and publisher have exhaustively
researched all sources to ensure the accuracy and
completeness of the information contained in this book, we
assume no responsibility for errors, inaccuracies, omissions
or any other inconsistency herein. Any slights against
people or organizations are unintentional.

For additional copies of this book, please see
the Quick Order Form in the back.

Attention colleges and universities, corporations, and
writing and publishing organizations: Quantity discounts
are available on bulk purchases of this book for educational
training purposes, fund-raising, or gift giving. Special
books, booklets, or book excerpts can also be created to fit
your specific needs. For information contact Marketing
Department, Aperneo@aperneo.com.

Dedication

I dedicate this book to many people, for many different reasons:

First, to the most unselfish and loving person I've ever met, Diane Olsen. She is the primary catalyst behind this book. Without her support and belief that I should give people the opportunity to read about the skills that have taken me more than thirty-five years to develop, you wouldn't be reading this book, and I wouldn't be fulfilling my purpose. She is my blessing, my buddy in life, and my best friend. I extend my deepest gratitude to her.

To our children, Gretchen, Courtney, Don, Connor and Tori—without you, I would have nothing to say. You've all taught me how to have the time of my life *right now*.

To my mother and father, whose love and support have never been in question. Dad, I know how proud you are of me, and Mom, you've always shown me what it means to hang on to a vision, regardless of the circumstances.

To Carol, my sister, who has taught my entire family what a gift from God truly means.

To Kevin Whalen, who personifies what's right about people, and has always believed in me.

To Mary Elizabeth Marx, for your random act of remarkable kindness.

Last, to you, the reader. You're living your life now, so why not do it on purpose and choose to '*have the time of your life*' while you're doing it.

Table of Contents

Prologue: A Letter From Larry Olsen

Why have I written this book?

In March 2000, I conducted a seminar in Houston. After the seminar, one of the participants approached me to tell me about the positive changes in her life. "Larry," she said, "this is the third time I've attended your program. It's about time I thanked you for saving my marriage."

"Thank you very much," I replied, "but I had nothing to do with saving your marriage. You're the one who should take the credit. You changed your perspective, and as a consequence, your marriage blossomed. From the sound of it, it seems like your decision to change was the right one."

She thought for a moment and continued, "That's why I'm thanking you. Until I attended this program and started applying the concepts to my own life, I tried to change everything and everyone around me. Instead of changing my perspective, I just kept trying to change my behavior. Your program showed me *how* to change, instead of *what* I should change into."

It was incredible to hear her story. It was powerful and touching, but it isn't entirely unique. The lessons in this book have had phenomenal effects on thousands of people's lives. Others have shared similar stories of success.

Another young man shared, "Larry, I've read so many books and tried so many different methods to make changes in my life. Until I understood your message, I didn't realize that simply wanting change, or trying method after method, will not create long-term change. The temporary changes I experienced just made me feel worse about myself, because they never lasted. I now know that beliefs drive behavior. Your program and its easy-to-use process has finally turned on the light for me. Thank you from the bottom of my heart."

"Thank you," I said. "It feels wonderful to know that your perspective is renewed. Always remember to be clear about what you want, because that's exactly what you'll get when you apply these lessons."

Once, a seminar attendee stopped me on my way out the door. "Larry, Larry, I know you need to go, but I want to tell you what has changed for me." I firmly believe that no matter how rushed we are, there are certain circumstances that merit spending extra time. From the look on this man's face, this was one of those times.

"I'd be glad to hear your story," I said.

He said, "The first time I attended your seminar, I must admit, I was rather negative. I wanted to be successful, but I then believed my obstacles were huge. I hadn't been in the country very long, my English was difficult to understand, and I wasn't as young as I thought you needed to be, to be successful.

"I am in sales, and taking time out from sales to attend a seminar—especially when I couldn't even make ends meet—was the last thing I needed. I only went because my employer strongly suggested that I attend—so I wasn't very open-minded.

"But after a while, I started to realize that this wasn't just another training session about how to do a better job or how to be a better person. Your program was all about *me*—how I think, and how if something isn't working for me, it will never get me ahead in life, no matter how hard I try. Until I learned this new lesson, I kept relying on my old ways.

"So guess what happened? I applied your lessons in my own life, and I not only became the top salesperson—I'm now the general manager!" He beamed, adding, "Thank you so much for sharing what you've discovered over the years, and for keeping it so simple that I could begin applying it to my life immediately."

After hearing this man's story and so many others, all I can feel is pure humility. I knew that I hadn't changed their lives; instead, it was the ideas that I had shared. Before I answer that question—"Why write this book?"—I'll share one more story.

A gentleman approached me once after hearing a number of people tell me about how their lives had changed for the better. "Larry," he said, "is this the first time you've heard powerful stories like these?"

"No," I replied. "I am blessed to hear them daily. Why do you ask?"

"Well," he said, "my name is Al. In addition to my career as a sales trainer, I have been a student of the human mind and the role it plays on our behavior. But in all my years of experience, I have never encountered anything like your L.I.F.E. program."

I thanked him, but wondered aloud what his point was.

"Just this," Al replied. "These lessons absolutely transform people. You know that, and I know that. The problem is, your corporate clients and their employees are the only ones who are lucky enough to be exposed to it. Everyone who applies what you teach finds positive change as a result—anything from doubling their income to living a more healthy life. More importantly, they become human *beings* rather than human *doings*, as you like to say.

"The point is, since you're the only one who knows what you know, what happens when you're gone? What happens to your life's work? Don't you think your work is important enough to make a permanent record of it? I think you need to stop thinking about your next seminar and start thinking about your first book."

I was shocked. I thought, "Who, me? Write a book? No way. I just haven't got the time." But as time went on, I started thinking about the success that people have experienced, and the importance of documenting it. I thought that perhaps it was time, after all. It wasn't that I didn't have the time, it was how I was choosing to use my time.

My challenge, however, was not whether I should do it or not, but whether I was the one to do it. I know my limitations—what I can and can't do. (Ever hear yourself say that?) Even though I agreed with the concept, I didn't start the book right away. Instead, I rationalized: "Hey, I'm not going to die anytime soon, I can always get it done. As soon as I get the time, I'll get started." With that mindset, I'd never get anything done. Every time I thought about starting the project, I'd think about all the work that lay ahead and talk myself out of it. Such thinking is very dangerous. In the mind, what is inherently doable can be turned into the impossible.

Several months after my encounter with Al, my wife and partner in life, Diane, and I decided to move to Bainbridge Island, which lies in Puget Sound just a thirty-minute ferry ride from Seattle. We'd spent three glorious years in Sugar Land, Texas, but we'd decided that the time had come to expand our business into the great American Northwest. Fortunately Diane's relentless persuasion won out over my procrastination until I was finally convinced that I did indeed need to write this book, and right away.

So I did, keeping one simple thought in mind: this information needed to be shared *right now*. Why? And why now? Because we are all here on this planet together. The better we feel about ourselves, the better we will treat each other. The better we treat each other, the more fun we will have, the more we will achieve, and the more fulfilled we will become. Dewitt Jones once said, "Be the best for the world, not the best in the world."

Think about it. Are you truly enjoying your life *right now*? Do others feel blessed to have known you? Are your children happy, self-confident, and glad that you are a part of their lives? Does your spouse or significant other ever come home early just to spend a few extra precious minutes with you? Are you in the best shape of your life so you can continue to be vibrant and strong for your children, your friends, and your family?

You see, *right now*, the present, is all we can guarantee. We can only hope for the future and try to put the past behind us, but the only place we will ever live is *now*. There is no other time—only this moment. This moment is where opportunity lives. Once we learn to discover each precious moment, it will provide us with all that is necessary for a truly inspired life.

So now you know why I finally decided it was time to write this book: to share the knowledge and valuable lessons I learned so you can embrace this one very precious and special life that you have, right here, *right now*.

Section One

BEGINNING THE
JOURNEY

An Introduction to L.I.F.E.

L et me ask you a simple, but important, question: are you having the time of
your life, right here, *right now*?

Not many people I meet answer "yes" to that question. For years, I couldn't say
"yes," either.

Now let me ask you something else: if you're not having the time of your life right
here, *right now*, would you like to? Would you like to learn how you can realize
your full potential as a human being, and along the way achieve untold joy and
create an immeasurable amount of joy in the lives of others? Would you like to
learn how to double your results, in half the time, and have twice the fun doing it?

I've got exciting news for you. I've been studying the cognitive, or thinking,
side of science and psychology for more than forty-five years as part of my work
in the corporate education business. I've helped countless others achieve more
joy and meaning in their lives. Through this vast experience and study, I've
developed a set of principles that, once you understand and apply them, will
transform your life.

At the core of these principles is what I call Lessons in the Fundamentals of
Excellence (L.I.F.E.^{sm}). Some of these ideas are thousands of years old, and
others are brand new. Together, these lessons will radically change the way you
think about yourself and the world around you.

I've been giving L.I.F.E. seminars all over the country for years now.
Thousands

of people from all walks of life have been positively affected by these simple, life-changing principles. For the first time, I've put as much as possible about this L.I.F.E. program in the pages of this book. It's here, waiting for you to read, absorb, and apply in your own life.

Please note: these L.I.F.E. lessons are *not* motivational. Motivational material, in my opinion, has its place, but it's a temporary bandage on a bigger problem, and little more than a short-term fix. After a day or two, you're almost always back to where you were before.

What I offer you instead is the opportunity to achieve long-term growth. You will be able to literally transform who you are, as we explore the way you think. Motivational materials are like chameleons, changing their color to adapt to their surroundings. I am going to help you become a caterpillar that transforms into the most beautiful butterfly.

How does this transformation happen? It happens through your thinking, which creates your attitudes, which in turn drives your behavior. These LIFE lessons will help you understand *how* you think and how you can change your thinking in a way that will change your life. It's just as Albert Einstein once said:

> "We can't solve problems by using the same kind of thinking we used when we created them."

You will learn how the "current you" thinks, and how your existing attitudes have been created. Next, you will learn how to change your thinking—which in turn will change your attitudes. Attitude is the key here; if you don't have a good attitude, you can't have a clear vision of what you want to accomplish. Without a clear, compelling vision, you won't achieve the success that you want and deserve in life.

Through these L.I.F.E. lessons, I'll show you how to not only create a new vision for yourself, but also how to make vision statements work in your life. These vision statements will help you experience everything you've always wanted out of life and will lead to a happier, more fulfilled you. I'll explain the Four Attitudes of Life, describe the Excellence Formula, list the S.T.E.P.S.^{sm} to success, and show you what I mean when I say that "my life ROX!"

You're probably thinking, "Larry, is it really that simple?"

The simple answer is yes. Change your thinking, and you'll change your life. It's happened to me, and I've seen it happen to thousands of other people. And because it has never failed anyone who has applied the concepts, I know it can happen to you.

Before we begin, I must stress one important point: I'm not going to tell you *what* to become, *what* to do, or *what* visions you should or shouldn't pursue. The answers to those questions are up to you; only you know your true essence—what's in your "heart of hearts." I can only give you the tools and the understanding that will allow you to achieve whatever you want to achieve, and become whoever you want to become.

Are you ready to experience the most incredible years of your life…starting *right now*? We all recognize that we only have one shot at life, whether or not we're willing to admit it. Life consists of a series of moments. How we embrace each of these moments determines whether or not we prosper, and if we achieve excellence or mediocrity. Absorb these lessons and apply them to your life, and you will be well on your way to a joyful existence that is presently beyond your grasp.

Always remember that you don't have to become someone else, someone extraordinary, to learn and apply these lessons. Why? It's simple—because you are already extraordinary *right now*. As this journey progresses, you'll understand how incredible you already are. This may be very difficult for you to believe. Most of us have been conditioned by others over time to believe that we're too thin, too fat, too slow, too poor, or too…whatever…to achieve our highest potential. Others dump expectations on us that have more to do with limiting our performance than maximizing it.

Guess what? Those expectations are flat-out wrong! You already possess everything you need *right now* to make your life the masterpiece it can be. All you have to do is begin. So please, let me welcome you to life: the one you've had, the one you're having *right now*, and the one you're about to begin!

As always, I am excited about life and thrilled about what is to come for you…and for me.

Larry Olsen,
Washington State

Getting the Most
From This Book

B efore we delve into the L.I.F.E.^{sm} lessons, I want to offer several suggestions to help you get the most out of this material.

Suggestion 1: When you see something you want to remember or refer to later, highlight it.

According to neuroscientists, two areas of the human brain primarily control behavior:

1. The amygdala, or reptilian brain
2. The cerebral cortex

The reptilian brain is our basic survival mechanism; it allows us to breathe, digest food, and so on. Fight-or-flight instincts are also located in the reptilian brain. The cerebral cortex enables us to reason, which separates us from animals. The reptilian brain handles our most essential day-to-day needs, but the more we use the cerebral cortex, needless to say, the better our lives will be.

The cerebral cortex has a left and a right hemisphere. When you are learning, you are typically using the left side of the brain. (Remember "left for logic" if you want to keep things simple.) The right hemisphere ("right for rhythm") is our creative side. It processes information like color and music.

We use the left side of our brains to understand abstract concepts like letters, and learn the meanings behind them. Educators have found that a learning environment that involves the right side of the brain at the same time as the left enhances a learner's ability to recall information. Thus, highlighting words with a color involves both the right and left hemispheres of your cerebral cortex.

So that's my suggestion: with a highlighter, mark the words, sentences, or paragraphs relevant to your experience or to which you want to refer later. The color doesn't matter. Use your highlighter as you read, because every time you physically interact with the information, you etch that new information into your brain. It's very important to be involved during the learning process, and highlighting words and passages will help you stay involved and increase your ability to absorb and retain what you're about to learn.

Suggestion 2: Listen to music as you read.

You can also stimulate the right side of your brain with music. This may be a bit contrary to most of the educational experiences that you've had. The ultimate learning environment most of us experienced in school was the library. When you walked into the library, what was the one word you associated with the ultimate learning environment? That's right—*silence*.

But here's the thing: what do you hear in a completely quiet environment? You hear *everything*. Unless you are so completely engulfed in your project that you can shut out all distractions, you may easily lose focus in a completely quiet place.

Music in the background can help you focus. Now, I don't recommend that you crank up your favorite pop tunes. Listening to music that you're already familiar with will take you somewhere else mentally. The lyrics or your memory of the song will stimulate associations in your mind. Once that happens, you're lost.

Instead, play some slow instrumental music, such as piano. Keep the music low, too. Music played too loud will be more of a distraction than no music at all.

Suggestion 3: Reread this material on a regular basis.

Many of us only retain about a quarter of the information we read. To prevent this, reread this material again and again to fully absorb and understand it. Highlighting certain sections and sentences, as mentioned earlier, will help you when you reread, as you can go directly to key passages and points.

How often should you review this book? At the beginning, I'd say at least once a week. Later, when the L.I.F.E. lessons are more fully incorporated into your daily thinking and routine, you may need only a periodic review. Just understand that you won't be able to "get" everything the first time. (I am confident that you *will* get just what you need.) To get the most out of these lessons, review them as often as you can.

Answering the
Prosperity Question

Ask yourself this question: Are you prosperous?

Now here's another question: how could you answer that question if I didn't first give you my definition of prosperity? That's right—you used your own definition. Before I tell you how I'm using the term, let me tell you what prosperity isn't.

Prosperity isn't happiness. Happiness is a by-product. Prosperity is not wealth. Wealth is a by-product. Prosperity isn't being in great physical shape, either; it's a by-product too.

Here's my definition of prosperity:

> You are prosperous if you are honestly able to say this:
> *I'm having the time of my life RIGHT NOW!*

You are the only person who can make that determination. No one else can say if you're prosperous or not. Now, how do most people live their lives? Most think that they'll be prosperous at some future point. Very few believe they're prosperous *right now*. When I ask people during my seminars if they're prosperous *right now*, I get these looks like they're thinking, "Larry, come on! Be real! I'm sitting in a seminar. I'm listening to you. Can you pick another time?"

You see, if you're not able to say that you're having the time of your life *right now*, then you're living in the future. You may preface most of your statements with, "Once I..." or "As soon as I..." Worse yet, you may be dwelling on how nice something was in the past or will be in the future.

Businesses are the same way. "Wow, as soon as we do this... As soon as the economy turns... As soon as we make the month... As soon as ... ."

Then what? Then you can say, "Yeeessss, that feels awesome!" Have you ever experienced that incredible "Yeeessss!" feeling when something went well for you? Has your child ever come up to you, looked you in the eye, and said, "I love you," for no other reason but to say so? Has someone ever approached you at work to say, "I'm so glad you're here, and we're so fortunate to have you on our team?"

Aren't we all searching for a way to positively impact our own lives and the lives of others? Unfortunately, that great feeling we get when someone says something nice about us only lasts for a few moments. And what do most people do when they receive a compliment? They become automatically humble: "Aw, shucks, don't be silly. It wasn't just me. Nope, I didn't have that much to do with it. Shucks. Gosh." They discount the compliment almost immediately. It's savored for a few moments, and then it's gone.

Disney World provides a great example of what most people are doing with their lives. What do Disney World and life have in common? If we don't know any better, they both teach us how to wait. Visitors to Disney World often stand in line for hours to experience a sixty-second ride. People will work all year for a two-week vacation there, and then they'll spend the whole time waiting. Life can become a waiting game if you don't learn about and embrace how incredible you are now. Many people wait for "Once I..." or "As soon as I.... " They truly believe that only *then* will they arrive. Why isn't the "as soon as" going on now? And "once I" *what*?

Have you ever noticed how long that moment we've all been striving for lasts? If you are like most people, it lasts about twenty seconds. By the time you've said, "Aw, it was nothing" or "I couldn't have done it without my team," the moment is gone. Do you know that during the average individual's lifetime, he or she will have only about thirty minutes of incredible feelings of accomplishment and satisfaction? Only thirty minutes of *"Yeeessss!"* For me, that's not enough!

You must first feel great about yourself *before* you can even think about positively impacting the lives of others—let alone your own. One of the many benefits of this style of living is your health. When you're feeling good about yourself, you don't get sick. Think about it: you never get sick when you're having the time of your life. When you get "down," however, your immune system is weaker. "Oh, I'm getting the sniffles now. It must be a cold. I get one every February." And your body thinks, "Okay, let's give him a cold."

When should you be experiencing prosperity, and having the time of your life? *Right now.* You can't wait. Remember those who live for "Once I..." or "As soon as this happens, then I'll..." are waiting for the right moment rather than turning *right now* into the right moment. Life is happening *to them*; they are not happening *to life.*

Most of us fall into this trap of waiting for a "moment" to come. Why? We're still "fixing" ourselves, tweaking who we are, what we can do, and what we know. We're still getting ready for the future.

Remember how simple it used to be? When you were a kid, if you wanted to play, you'd knock on a friend's door and ask, "Hey, you wanna come out and play?"

Your friend would respond, "Yeah!"

"Great! Let's go!" And then you'd go play. Simple.

If I came over to your house tomorrow, knocked on your door, and asked you to come out and play, you'd probably say, "Uhh, what do you plan on playing, Larry? Approximately how long will we be engaged in this endeavor? There are a few people I have to check with first, of course. In fact, we're gonna have to have a meeting about it before I can come out and play."

Studies have shown that when people are having fun, they're more productive. They're not more productive when they're throwing things around, yelling at coworkers, or pounding on a machine. They're more productive when they're having fun at what they're doing *no matter what it is that they're doing.* You'd agree with those studies, wouldn't you?

You must ask yourself: "If I'm not having the time of my life, when should I have it?"

The answer, of course, is *right now!* Life happens now—not at some future point. If you come up to me and say, "Larry, are you having the time of your life?" I'll go, "Yes! Thank you for asking." So now do you want to come out and play?

I'm Not *Smart* Enough

So what do you need to begin having the time of your life *right now?*

First, you must give yourself permission to arrive, so to speak. In your gut, you must realize that it doesn't get any better than you, *right now.* Now, this doesn't mean that you're better than everybody else; it simply means you don't have to be better than anyone else, and that no one else is better than you. Your entire focus should be on what you're capable of becoming and achieving.

During my seminars and coaching sessions, I've had a lot of people give me some variation of this statement: "It's too late in the game for me to change my thinking. I'm not smart enough to be prosperous now." I've had people explain to me, in depth, that the poor grades they received in school were "proof" of how dumb they were. Grades aren't a measure of intelligence; they only indicate how interested a person is in the subject. That's all. Have you ever noticed how well you did at the things you were really interested in?

Let me fill you in on a little secret:

> You are already excellent.
> In fact, you're already a GENIUS!

Have you ever told another person, "Oh, by the way, I'm a genius?" You should, because you'd be right. Many years ago, neuroscientists believed that you and I had more than ten billion neurons in our brains. Each neuron is capable of processing millions of bits of information. When scientists and mathematicians tried to establish how many patterns were possible among the interactions of these various neurons, they found that it wasn't finite. An infinite number of patterns were possible. That means what's possible for us is limitless.

With the use of electron microscopes, neuroscientists found that they had been mistaken—humans didn't have ten billion neurons after all. At a minimum, humans have a hundred billion neurons. How do you get a handle on a huge number like that and why should you, because it begins the process of knowing why we can go beyond what we currently think is possible. I've found the easiest way to do so is to compare these numbers with something we're all familiar with—time. We all have an excellent handle on time. Here's a little story that puts these numbers into perspective.

My son Don came home from preschool one day and asked if I'd like to hear him count to one hundred in seconds. He was very proud of the fact that he could count that high and was going to do the "one Mississippi, two Mississippi" thing. I figured he'd be done in about a minute and a half, so I said sure, let me hear it. After he finished, I told him I was proud of him, and off he went. A few months later, Don told me he could count to a million, and asked if I wanted to hear it. I asked him if he was going to do that "one Mississippi, two Mississippi" thing again. He said he was, and asked if we could get started.

"Don, I'd love to hear you count to a million, but do you have any idea how long that would take?"

"No, Daddy, how long?"

I said, "One million seconds is eleven and a half days."

His response was, "Then let's get started."

Remember, each neuron can process millions of bits of information. Counting to one billion would take almost thirty-two years. We have a minimum of one hundred billion neurons. Is that huge or what? Are you ready for a trillion seconds? A trillion seconds is thirty-two thousand years. All that potential is compressed into a three-pound miracle in your head!

So every one of us has, at a minimum, a hundred billion neurons—if not more. And do you know what else is amazing? Scientists have found that the smartest among us only use anywhere from eight to fifty percent of their neurons.

See why you're a genius? The brain is an amazing thing. Many, including myself, consider it the last great frontier; we are finding out that tiny space inside each of our heads may be as large as outer space in terms of what it contains.

Now let me ask you this: if the brightest people in the world are said to be using only eight to 50 percent of their neurons, do you think you have any room for growth? Is there anything that you couldn't handle mentally? Of course not.

You are a genius.

I know what you might be thinking. Perhaps you have had a rather checkered past. You've partied hard. Yes, if you've drunk a significant amount of alcohol, you've lost a few brain cells. But the percentage you've lost—compared to what you still have available—is tiny. It would be like taking a cup down to the beach, scooping out a glassful of ocean water every day, and tossing the water onto the beach. Will the ocean be empty in your lifetime? Not even close.

You have no excuse for talking yourself out of excellence. The only reason you may not feel like a genius is that you were taught to believe information about yourself that wasn't true. Just because someone else believes something about you doesn't make it true. What the L.I.F.E. lessons will prove, however, is that if you believe what others have told you, it does becomes your truth. What do you believe is your truth, in every area of your life? Is that truth holding you back, or setting you free?

I'm Not That Good

Another attitude I've run across over the years is a variation on the theme, "I'm not good enough to succeed."

Don't determine who you are by the mistakes you've made. You tried your best. You didn't fail or make mistakes on purpose. The people who are most able to succeed accept their weaknesses alongside their strengths. Don't beat yourself up over what you've done poorly. Know that you will have an unlimited amount of opportunities to change and grow.

It's all about attitude. Skills are important, but they will only take you so far. You must also possess a great attitude. A person with great skills and a bad attitude won't be successful. I know what you're thinking now: oh, brother, here comes the "great attitude" thing again. But how do you get a "great attitude" or change a bad one if it's standing in your way of prosperity? Well, if you're interested in learning how to change an attitude, from one that is holding you back to one that will literally accelerate your growth, you're reading the right book.

It doesn't matter how many challenges you're facing *right now*, either. You may have a stack of bills to pay, a too-demanding boss, or some sort of physical ailment. You can overcome *anything* with the right attitude and the right behavior.

You may be thinking, "That's easy for you to say, Larry. You have your own business. You're successful—people fly you around the country first-class to hear you speak. You have a loving wife, and great kids."

Yes, but I overcame scores of challenges along the way, and will be confronted with more in the future. In fact, if you wanted to match up to see who has had the most challenges in their life, I'd take you on. One of my children died. I almost declared bankruptcy three times. (Trust me—when it comes to bankruptcy, "almost" is close enough.) I've been divorced, and my kids live in different cities. I've had phenomenally terrible things happen in my life. You and I could get our violins out, and by the time we were finished comparing how challenging our lives have been, we'd both still be right here, *right now*, facing our future, wouldn't we.

We are doing ourselves a disservice when we set limitations about what we can or can't accomplish. You and I are much more alike than we are different. We are all experiencing this precious moment we have *right now*. We are together in this moment, and the only thing that's different about us and our opportunities is not what happens to us, but how we've learned to talk to ourselves about what happens to us.

Don't do yourself a disservice by discounting what you can accomplish in life based on what you have or haven't been able to do up to this point. Don't let obstacles—large or small—talk you out of working toward and ultimately achieving your visions.

A Final Note

Are you prosperous?

Some of you may be thinking, *"Yes, I am."* If that's the case, you may be wondering if this book is worth reading. If everything in your life is great *right now*, then you should think of yourself as a world-class athlete. The difference between first and second in world-class athletics can be just a hundredth of a second, but it is the difference between first and second. You're reading this book to "tweak" yourself. Remember, at most, the best and smartest people in the world are using half of their potential. If everything is great and you're pumped about who you are in every area of your life, that's outstanding. You've got to want to change for your reasons, and your reasons alone. But never forget: if you don't change now, a year from now you'll only be a year older.

If you want to find out if this book can be your catalyst for transformation, ask yourself these questions:

1. Are there any current challenges that I'm facing in my life *right now*, that, if I were able to find a way to change them, would improve the quality of this very precious and special life that I have?

2. Do I have any visions or goals for my life that I haven't accomplished yet? Are there any that I've talked myself out of, for any reason? If I could find a way to accomplish them in half the time with twice the fun, would that be worth taking the time to read and apply the information in this book?

If you've answered "yes," to either or both questions then the L.I.F.E. lessons will help you prosper in life, up to and beyond your wildest expectations.

Section Two

LESSONS IN THE
FUNDAMENTALS OF
EXCELLENCE

Lesson 1: The Genius Within Wants Out

" There is nothing arrogant about the truth; it's anything less that limits us." — Larry Olsen

When you finish reading this book, you will join one percent of the world's population—the one percent that actually knows *how* it thinks. The other 99 percent think about whatever happens to be on their minds, whether it's good for them or not. What many of us don't know is that *we have become who we are based on the thinking that we have accumulated along the way.*

You're also going to recognize that only one person controls your experience in life—you. Have you ever noticed that you're the only one who can see things from your perspective? That wherever you go, you're always there? You are also the only one who knows how you are doing in every area of your life!

It's worth pointing out that none of us are immortal. We all have the opportunity now to experience life to the fullest, yet sometimes things "happen to us" and prevent us from succeeding. Most of us would like to believe that we're proactive— that we happen to life, rather than the other way around. But that rarely happens if you don't know the power of your own thinking.

Why is that? Our minds have been conditioned to think a certain way, and our behaviors follow our attitudes. Did you know that approximately seventy billion people have walked upright in the history of this planet Earth? Currently you are one among seven plus billion people. No two of these people have had exactly the same genetic blueprint or fingerprint. We're all different. We're all unique. Not only are we unlike anyone else—we're not *supposed* to be like anyone else. You and I are at our absolute best when we are our own magnificent selves, but we live in a society that attempts to make us all the same. We've become so used to believing that all we have to do is "show up" and let things happen that we usually just respond automatically, whether the situation is good or bad.

Have you ever asked yourself how much of your thinking affects you as an individual? How much control do you have over your own thoughts? Are you maximizing the opportunities that your brain presents to you? No. At best, you and I are just scratching the surface of what's possible for us, but some of us have scratched so long that we now have a firm grip on our lives. The good news is this: your attitude, rather than your knowledge or experience, determines your ultimate success. But your knowledge and experience created your attitude.

Does that sound like a *Catch-22*? Are you thinking, "I'm right back where I started from?" Not really. The answer to prosperity lies in becoming aware of your own thinking and its power to create, and then learning how to control your thinking. Why? *Because if we don't learn how to control our own thinking, our thinking will control us.*

And that really is the focus of the L.I.F.E. message: *you can control your thinking, and thus transform your own life!* But to accomplish that, you've got to leave some old attitudes behind. You'll see how easy this is once you fully understand how to affect your own thinking. It's not difficult. In fact, many people struggle with how simple it is. If I had known how easy it is to change, I would have done it years ago they say. We've been taught that life is a struggle, and the vast majority of people still believe that.

After one of my seminars, a very intelligent gentleman approached me and said, "Larry, I've been studying how the mind works most of my life. It just can't be this easy." He was struggling with the L.I.F.E. message's simplicity because it contradicts most of what he had learned about change.

I said, "Well, would you like me to make it more difficult?

"No," he responded. "The simpler, the better."

As you're going to find out, the more you understand how your brain works, the easier it is to positively affect your thinking and transform your behavior without working hard at it. We have a tendency to complicate things—sometimes for our own validation. What I'm talking about is simple. It all begins with understanding how you've been thinking in the past and how you can think more effectively in the future, while experiencing phenomenal benefits *right now*.

We're going to talk a lot about attitudes, and we're going to talk a lot about having great vision. Don't get put off by the word "vision." It's also a simple concept. I will be talking about setting and accomplishing visions rather than about setting and accomplishing goals. The reason for that is simple: goals are simply steps to the vision. The vision is the *why*, and the goal is the *how*. For example, you might have a goal of getting your weight down to 150 pounds so you can achieve your vision of being a lean, keen, change-agent machine.

When we start examining the process of creating and accomplishing visions, we will begin by thinking more in the short term than in the long term. Why? Because the average individual can't visualize more than three months into the future, but we're going to change that. Think it's difficult? It's not, *once you know how.* Let me give you a quick example: if you want incredible children, when should you begin seeing them as incredible? *Right now!*

I Want You to Sing a Song

I want you to pretend that you're in a room full of people you know, and I'm leading the group. Suddenly, I ask you to come up and sing a song to the entire group. "In a moment, you're going to sing a song."

Let's look into this a little deeper and see what took place from a physiological perspective. When I asked you to come up and sing a song, I sent audio waves through the air. Those audio waves were diverted by those little flaps of skin on the side of your head called ears. They entered the ear and caused the eardrum to vibrate. The vibration traveled along the bones of the middle ear to the cochlea, causing the hair cells inside to bend and stimulate sensory nerve fibers. (Are you still with me?) Then the fibers translated the vibrations to electrical impulses, which immediately traveled to the auditory cortex. At that point, you instantly experienced an attitude. An attitude is simply a learned behavior. You aren't born with attitudes—you learn them throughout your life.

Now, what's really interesting about how we operate is that before you became aware of the attitude, you emotionalized. Scientists have found that humans are in a constant state of emotion. Based on your attitude, you talked to yourself about the emotion, and based on the emotions that were created by your pre-existing attitude, you began to make up your mind about how you felt about singing a song.

Our attitudes, in other words, influence how we feel about things. Perhaps you're thinking, "Larry, that's true, but only to a certain extent. There are other factors involved." Are you certain? What percentage of your performance do you think is based on your attitude? Seventy-five percent? Ninety-five percent? Ninety-eight percent?

The truth is, it's 100 percent of your performance. Attitudes, in other words, don't *kind* of affect our behavior. Attitudes affect 100 percent of our behavior.

Do you see how important attitude is to your behavior, which in turn affects your performance? For most people what you get from life is based more on what you put into it (conditioning) than what you want to get out of it (visions).

The process I just described—the sound waves going through the air into your ears, becoming electrical impulses, and creating emotions from attitudes or starting the process of creating a new attitude—all takes place faster than you and I can think about it. The brain operates very rapidly. What do I mean by *rapidly*? Sound travels at approximately 760 miles per hour, or 1,100 feet per second. The brain processes information at approximately 720,000 miles an hour or 12,000 miles per second. It takes the conscious mind anywhere from a half of a second to a second and a half to react to the decision you subconsciously already made. (You may want to read that again.)

Remember, attitude is a pre-determined response to a given stimulus. If the stimulus is "sing a song," the response is an attitude. Did you know that it's a synaptic electrochemical reaction between the axons and dendrites of the neurons that makes up thinking to begin with? Your conscious mind takes anywhere from a half a second to a second and a half to pay attention to the decisions you've already made so you can behave *appropriately*.

"Appropriately" is the key word. What do I mean when I say that? Appropriate to what? Appropriate to the preconceived attitudes stored within your brain. In other words, your attitudes don't always lead to the best behavior. We've been conditioned to think a certain way.

> *"Well, I've always been that way."*

> *"Oh, my dad was like that."*

> *"I learned that from my mother."*

My response to those comments is this: "No kidding?" I mean, who were your models? Who were your mentors? Who were the individuals who were instrumental in your life? In any twenty-four hour period, humans have approximately 50,000 thoughts going on in their minds, or one thought every 1.7 seconds. You will discover that thoughts accumulate to build beliefs or attitudes. In other words, we make up our minds about our behavior all the time based more on what has *already happened to us* rather than what is *possible for us*.

Who or what has given us these preconceived attitudes? Here are a few:

- Parents
- Siblings
- School
- Church
- Friends
- Community
- Bosses

- Work colleagues

- Television

- Rox-Talk™, which I'll explain later

Do you see that who you are is a result of preconceived attitudes you learned over time from yourself and others? You can change this way of thinking, however, and when you change your thinking, you can move from "Who am I?" to the real question—"Who can I become?"

The genius inside you, in other words, wants out. Only you can let the genius out.

Your Attitude and Performance

When I asked you to come up and sing a song in front of everyone, you most definitely had one of the following four attitudes.

Attitude 1: No way!

When I said, "I'd like you to sing a song," many of you thought, "Like hell I'm going to sing a song!" In other words, you thought, "I'm in no danger of singing a song. I'm an adult now, and I can say no."

What do you think these people's attitudes are about themselves as singers? They probably don't think they're any good. Why? Fear. The most common fear among people is the fear of rejection. Singing in front of a group is an opportunity to be rejected, so fear kicks in; anyone who has this fear probably won't sing.

The second most common fear is the fear of change. That's why my message is so powerful, because we all know the only thing you can count on is change. It is the only consistent thing. People adjust most easily to changes they came up with themselves, particularly if they have identified the value of making these changes. Learning how to change can easily eliminate much of the stress in our lives.

The third most common fear is the fear of death. (This fear moves up to number one once you find out your death is imminent and you don't feel prepared.) Doesn't this show you how powerful the first two fears are? People would rather die than change or be rejected!

Attitude 2: Can't wait!

These folks are excited; they *want* to sing. They might ask, "Will there be a microphone? Are more people coming?"

How do you think these people see themselves as singers? They probably think they're pretty good. (Or at least they're not intimidated by coming up in front of a group.) Their attitudes will let them succeed. They're ready.

You're probably already beginning to see the power of attitude. When your attitude is positive, you'll probably be successful. Things that you have a positive attitude about just seem to come easily to you. Can you begin to imagine what would take place in your life if you were able to change your attitudes? Take a moment, if you will, and jot down a few of your positive attitudes. Then jot down some of the attitudes that you would like to change. Would there be any value to your life if you could change the negative attitudes that are holding you back? What would those values be?

Positive attitudes:

_____

_____

_____

_____

Negative attitudes:

_____

_____

_____

_____

Values received if negative attitudes changed:

_____

_____

_____

_____

_____

_____

Attitude 3: Indifference

The people with this attitude would get up in front of the group and sing, but they'd be less than excited about it. They'd go through the motions, and sit down. They'd be indifferent to the whole experience.

This third response stems from the attitude that's most difficult to overcome, not only in ourselves but also in others. Many of us go through life this way. As we discussed previously, change is difficult. A lot of what you're going to learn from this book are things that you already know in your heart, but I'm going to put them in a little different perspective. We are simply tweaking our perspective.

Pay attention, for a moment, to what the third person is saying:

"What'd he say?"

"He said we're gonna sing."

"Oh. Do we have to?"

"I don't know, nobody's come up yet. Will you if you have to?"

"I guess."

"Do you want to?"

"No."

That's indifference. Indifference is when you anesthetize yourself to feel anything emotionally. We've all experienced that at times in our lives. When you take an indifferent person to a movie, do they have any fun?

"Hey, do you want go to a movie tonight?"

"Yeah, I'd love to. What do you want to see?"

"I don't care."

"Let's go see the new Bruce Willis movie, I hear it's great!"

"Nah, he's too intense. Is there anything else playing?"

"Well, yeah. What would you like to see?"

"I don't care."

Indifference is difficult to overcome.

Attitude 4: Having a vision

This fourth response is what this book is about. These people see singing in front of the group as an opportunity and choose how to respond.

Let's talk about visions. We've all heard the term "vision." We all have visions. What I'd like to do is to give you some clear distinctions between goals and visions, which aren't the same things. Our society is goal-oriented. Many goal-oriented people have created more "have tos" than "want tos" in their lives. This is one major reason why many people have limited their success.

Vision is different. People with vision think: "I look forward to new opportunities and seize them with enthusiasm and excitement!" When I said, "I'd like you to sing a song in front of the entire group," the people with vision thought, "What?" and experienced an attitude, just like everyone else. But instead of being stuck *reacting* to the new situation based on an old attitude, they *intervened* in the stimulus/response process by saying the following: "Wait a minute—is this is an opportunity? Am I enthusiastic and excited?"

Next, their attitude took over, as it always does. It's etched into the neurons—a "no-brainer," if you will, because it's already been pre-programmed. But the difference is that people with vision first think, "Wait a minute—is this an opportunity?" and then they respond with the vision rather than the old attitude. If you don't have the vision, you are stuck with the old attitude.

We all have the power of choice regarding how we think about something. People with a vision have a choice now. They're choosing the new experience *based on a vision of what could be*, instead of choosing the new experience *based on the past.*

The brain is miraculous, isn't it? How can you get an attitude that's going to affect your performance 100 percent based on something you haven't even done yet? What would happen if you already knew how to behave, no matter the circumstances? Can you imagine anybody behaving like that? Think about it.

"Honey, we're going to a party tonight."

"Where are we gonna go? What're they gonna serve? Who's gonna be there?"

"Why do you want to know?"

"Well, I want to know what kind of an attitude to put on before we go."

Later, after dinner, you might think, "I knew I wouldn't have any fun, because so-and-so was there again," or, "I knew I'd have a great time, because so-and-so was there again!" It doesn't matter what the event is. If we don't know any better, we bring an attitude to a party without even knowing it, and the party will happen to us instead of us happening to the party.

So how could you possibly make up your mind about how singing a song was going to be before you've even done it? Past experience, right? We've all sung before, haven't we? You have an idea of what kind of singer you are, and that idea affects how you feel about what's about to take place.

> Internally, we predetermine success or failure.

How many attitudes do we have? Most people have thousands. What's an attitude? It's a learned behavior. You must learn how to change your thinking if you ever hope to change your attitudes.

I know some readers might be thinking, "That's not me, Larry. I'm open-minded." Wrong! Did you know that "open-minded" is an oxymoron—an example of two words that don't work together?

Why is open-minded an oxymoron? Because you're only open to what you agree with, and nothing else. You might be thinking, "No, no, no! I'll listen to opinions I don't agree with!" That may be true, but you're always listening to the conversation inside your head while you're listening to someone else. On the outside you're thinking, "Oh, that's really fascinating," but on the inside, you're thinking, "This person's out of his mind!" We might listen and politely nod our heads to another person's ideas, but if those ideas don't match our own belief system, it's extremely difficult to believe a word he or she is saying.

Stress and Performance

Stress also plays a factor in performance. Have you ever heard this statement: "It's difficult to be confident if you're not competent?" Let me give you an example: the word "honey" doesn't mean what it could until you've actually tasted honey, right? Right. You can intellectualize it and imagine what honey might taste like, but until you've experienced it, it's nothing more than a word.

Pretend that you're back at the point where I've just asked you to sing in front of a group of people you know, and you're choosing the first attitude: *"No way am I singing in front of the group!"*

What's happening inside you *right now*? You don't see yourself as a singer or as someone who is comfortable standing in front of a group, but you're about to do just that. That's a contradiction, and the contradiction creates stress in your system. Your fight-or-flight mechanism kicks in. Your palms become moist, and your pulse rises. If I were to put a blood pressure cuff on you, you'd watch its gauge rise. Why? Your body's starting to restrict. Your heart beats faster and your vocal chords stretch. If you do begin to sing, you'll do so in a scratchy, sickly voice.

The number one killer in America today is not cancer. It's heart disease. Heart disease kills far more people than cancer, the majority of which is curable, by the way. But most people think, "Oh, my God—cancer!"

The number one cause of heart disease is not hardening of the arteries or too much cholesterol. Instead, it's stress, known as "the silent killer." Let's talk a little about stress. Stress floods your system with toxins that can slowly break down your internal systems—particularly the immune system. It's like a little cancerous activity that goes on. Now if I asked you to sing, and you assumed the first attitude—"No way!"—you may reduce your life expectancy by several hours, conservatively speaking, by exposing yourself to stress. You might be thinking, "Wait a minute—I don't want you taking several hours off my life!" Don't worry—with what you're about to learn, you'll add *years* to your life simply by being able to control your thinking and lower the stress in your life.

There is positive stress. It's called positive discontent. It's the same stress you experienced when you were a small child, excited about holiday gifts. Maybe you saw a present with your name on it, and begged your father: "Can I open a present, Dad? Please?" Your father probably told you something like, "No, but cheer up—you've only got a few more days." A few *days*? That's forever!

Here's something else that's interesting about stress. How did I cause you to feel stress when I asked you to sing the song? Audio waves, right? All I did was say, "In a moment, you're going to sing." If you didn't want to sing, your system was flooded with toxins. If you were looking forward to singing, your system was flooded with a wonderful chemical called endorphins. My words are only words. But they create feelings inside you. Think about the power of words.

Lock On/Lock Out

I want to expand on something I mentioned earlier in this chapter. We filter what we see, hear, taste, touch, and smell based on our preconceived attitudes. We all want to be correct, so we "lock on" to what we believe is true, and "lock out" everything else.

When we lock on to something mentally, we lock out all the other information and possibilities. You are doing this—unconsciously, most of the time—twenty-four hours a day. Think of honking cars and running engines; the hum of an air conditioner; visual noise, like billboards; and so on. You filter the vast majority of this information out.

Let me show you another example of lock on/lock out. You may have seen this drawing before; it's been around since the early 1900s. Look at the drawing until you see a woman.

Did you see a young woman or an old woman? (If you didn't see either, show it to someone else and ask him or her to show it to you. Some people only see black objects on white.)

Old woman or young lady?

Some people immediately see a young woman, and others see an old hag. Imagine that you are in a room of twenty people, and nineteen of those people see the young woman and only one sees the hag. Let's say that the young woman represents our goal or future opportunity. Can I develop an attitude about the one person who sees the hag? Of course. I'd probably think that that person is wrong. Why? *Because he or she doesn't agree with me and the rest of the group.*

First Impressions Last a Lifetime

It's easy to develop an attitude about someone who doesn't see things the way I do. A first impression is made in the blink of an eye. Those impressions can last a lifetime.

Imagine that I am the president of the company where you work, and I am illustrating prosperity to you by showing you and a group of your colleagues the picture of the woman. You look at the image and see the young woman. I say, "This is what prosperity looks like. Would you like to be a part of the most incredible month we have ever had and have the most prosperity you've ever experienced? Would there be any value in that for you?"

You nod your head, so I continue. "Fantastic! Let me show you what it looks like. For us, this month will be an old lady month! You can't wait, huh? Are you pumped? It's going to be awesome! Now go back to your department and get everybody excited!"

You nod your head and leave. You never saw the old lady, and you have no idea what I am talking about. Are you in on the vision? No way.

Why didn't you just say, "I don't get it?" More often than not, we see a person who objects, or even raises a question, as an antagonist. We think of that person as negative. They're not a "team player" by our definition. You'd rather say nothing at all than be perceived as negative.

But who is right? The people who see the old woman, or the people who see the young woman? Some people see both images. What about them?

When Is the Truth the Truth?

After the goal-setting meeting, the real meeting occurs—the meeting where employees talk about the meeting. The people who saw the hag get together and talk about the people who saw the young woman, and the people who saw the young woman talk about the people who saw the hag. Why? Because people are naturally attracted to people they agree with. But let's not forget about the third group, who see both the young woman *and* the hag; they don't understand how the rest of the people could possibly be so slow.

I'm sure that by now you see my point. Intellectually, we know that people who don't see or believe the same things we do are not necessarily wrong—they just have different conditioning than we do. But *emotionally*, our feelings may be quite the opposite.

I must be careful not to develop an attitude about someone just because she sees things differently than I do. Why? Because if I do, every time I see her I'll doubt her abilities. Every time she sees me, she will know that I don't see the best in her. How do you feel about being with people who don't see the best in you, and instead are focused on your shortcomings? How excited are you about their leadership?

Do you think it's possible to form opinions about people based on your impressions of them? Do you think that if I met you and you were having a bad day, I could form a fair opinion of you? What if you were having a good day? Could I form a fair opinion based on that? Of course I could. You could form an opinion of me based on what I've written, or even about the cover of this book, even though you haven't met me yet. Is that a good way to judge who I really am, any more than if I locked on to who you are based on the mood you were in when I first met you?

But if you don't have a vision, that's how you'll make first impressions. You think, "Don't confuse me with the facts. I've got my mind made up." Lock on/lock out is a fact, and if we don't know we are doing it, we think we know the truth. Once we think we know the truth, we are caught in another trap: *I'd rather be right than successful*. Subconsciously, you will always look for information to support your belief—whether it's good or bad.

Decide What They Are Like Before You Meet Them

Can we break the trap of locking on? You will never stop locking on, because it's the way you're wired. It's human nature. That being the case, I challenge those of you who want to be great leaders of yourselves or others (or excellent parents, wonderful friends, etc.) to do what I have learned how to do, which is to form your opinion about others *before* you meet them. Otherwise, you'll hang around with them for a while and then form your opinion.

Form an opinion first? That's crazy! But is it? Let me tell you a little story to explain my reasoning. I am well paid for what I do because any time an investment delivers a healthy return, the investor is happy. The more invested in what works, the greater the return. Fair enough? Now, I can develop attitudes with the best of them. But let's say a company asks me to help a particular employee who isn't reaching his potential, and that during my seminar, that person closes his eyes frequently. Do you think the attitude that I've formed about this "jerk" could affect my efforts spent with him? Of course it could!

If I go into the endeavor with a pre-conceived notion about this person, I will only look for information to support my belief. I will lock out any behavior that he exhibits that is not representative of a "jerk." The end result will be just as I expected—"How do you expect me to be successful with a jerk, anyway? I tried as hard as I could."

Being Your Best in Spite of the Circumstances

Therefore I am faced with a challenge. This company has paid dearly for my services, so is it fair for me to start things off with the wrong attitude about one of its employees? Will the company get a fair return on its investment? Absolutely not! But does this happen? Absolutely—in fact, it happens every single day.

What about you? Do you ever go to work with the wrong attitude? Have you ever worked alongside someone who did? Did that person's negative attitude affect your attitude? It's very hard to be "up" around people who are down.

So how do I resolve this challenge? Simple, I make my mind up about that employee *before I meet him*. That's right! Let me tell you what I have locked on to about you. You are a genius; you have over one hundred billion neurons; you're attractive, talented, and very forgiving; you're always looking for the best in others, and I can't think of anyone I'd rather spend time with than you. Now, if I sincerely believe these things and treat you that way, how will you treat me? That's correct—you'll treat me the same. This almost seems selfish, but I would rather have you treat me that way than get to know me for a while and then treat me according to whatever mood you happen to find me in.

You see, once I've locked on to how incredible you are and I see you fall asleep during my talk, it's easy for me to lock that out. Why? Because I know that you're not a jerk. You're probably just tired. Maybe I need to work harder to keep your attention. In either case, I'm going to choose to focus on what's *right* about you and treat you accordingly.

What have you locked on to about your children, spouse, co-workers, parents, and friends? Most importantly, what have you locked on to about yourself? Have you locked on to the attitude and behaviors that you want, or what they have become?

Can You Fake It Until You Make It?

There's something else that's important—something that makes it impossible for us to hide our true feelings. There's only one person you are in any danger of fooling—yourself. Everyone else can see right through you. You cannot "fake it till you make it."

Have you ever heard that body language and tone of voice account for about 90 percent of communication, and words only about 10 percent? An avid reader has several thousand words in their vocabulary, but the average person only uses a few thousand each day. If that's the case, in the battle of what we communicate, what wins every single time? If you put a few thousand warriors—words—on one side of the battle and over 200,000 warriors—body language and tone of voice—on the other, which side will win? Of course—body language and tone of voice! "Who you are speaks so loudly I can't hear what you're saying." Emerson. Body language and tone of voice are driven by beliefs, and that's why you can't fake it till you make it. The most powerful warrior is authenticity, because it cuts through anything. There is nothing purer than being yourself.

How Do You See Yourself?

Locking on is a physiological process that I'll explain In greater depth when we get to the next lesson. Just know that you are wired to lock on. What have you locked on to about yourself in the following areas?

- How you interact with your children

- How you and your spouse think about and treat each other

- How you listen to others

- How you think about your job or profession

- How much money you deserve

- How you think of yourself

- How you think other people see you

- How physically healthy you are

- How you consider yourself spiritually

- Whether you're able to be prosperous *right now*

Locking on is important. Right now, the hair follicles in your skin are sending thousands of messages to your brain. If you are paying attention to the weight of your clothing, there's no way you'd be able to read this book and get anything out of it. We have to screen information out. As you'll see in the next lesson, unfortunately, a lot of us are screening out prosperity.

What we must learn to do is to *lock on and open up*. When you meet someone new for the first time, remember: you don't know all there is to know about that person. In fact, as I shared with you earlier, you need to create an attitude about that person *before* you meet him.

- She has one hundred billion neurons plus

- She's attractive

- She's funny

- I'll find something of value in her to focus on

And so on. Now remember: this must be authentic. To be authentic, you must identify why it would be more advantageous to treat them in the new way rather than the old way. *What would it look and feel like if you started doing that to yourself?*

Scotomas

Why aren't we all succeeding in all areas of our lives? What does our current perception of the truth have to do with our ability to see what's possible for us instead of what has already happened to us? Let's find out.

Read the following passage one time to yourself. You'll understand why in just a minute.

> FINISHED FILES ARE THE RESULT
> OF YEARS OF SCIENTIFIC STUDY
> COMBINED WITH THE EXPERIENCE
> OF MANY YEARS.

Now, read this again and, without marking them, count how many Fs you see.

How many Fs did you see? When I do a seminar with, say, forty people, the results usually vary widely. Most people see two or three while a few see more. On rare occasions, someone might come up with the correct answer: six. Before reading further, review the passage again.

Most people find the Fs in "finished" and "files." A few will also pick up the F in "scientific." But what about the other three Fs? What will it take for me to prove to you that there are really six Fs in the above statement? I like to say that most of us come from Missouri—the "show me" state. With that state of mind, it's easy to believe that the truth only exists if I can see it. I'm not stupid, so show me.

But before I show you, allow me to share my Excellence Formula with you:

> Rather than working harder or smarter at what isn't working,
> THINK DIFFERENTLY and accomplish more.

Albert Einstein realized the importance of changing thinking instead of process. According to Einstein, "We can't solve problems by using the same thinking we used when we created them." Are you ready?

Look for the word "of." Now how many Fs do you see?

Why don't most of us see all six Fs the first time we read that passage? We've created a *scotoma*, which is a Greek word meaning "blind spot." The reason we may not have seen all of the Fs is because we have been conditioned not to. You and I were taught to sound out our words. Several years ago, my daughter Courtney took her first spelling test. Only four words appeared on the test, and she missed one of them: "of." She based its spelling on her phonetic conditioning: "ov," because that's how it sounds. Once we are conditioned a particular way, we develop scotomas to block out everything else.

Scotomas are troublesome precisely because *we don't know that we have them*. We think that what we see is the honest-to-God truth, what we experience is the truth, and what we witness is the truth. We give up too easily to our scotomas. What if you only found three Fs, I told you there were six, and you still couldn't find them? Have you ever said to yourself, "I can't find it, I don't get it, and I've never been good at that"? Your billions of neurons fail you when you say that. They're not going to provide you with any information, because you must be absolutely right about your *belief*—whether it's good for you or not.

All I Want Is Coffee

Several years ago, I had breakfast at a nice restaurant in Clearwater, Florida. I'd finished my meal and wanted some coffee, so I tried to flag down a waiter. We all have our own style of getting a waiter, don't we? First, I try to make eye contact. If that doesn't work, I speak up. I couldn't catch anyone's eye, so I finally said, "Excuse me." But none of the waiters heard me.

I wanted my coffee, and time was running out—I had an appointment. Pretty soon, I loudly exclaimed, "Excuse me! May I have some coffee?"

The entire restaurant fell silent. Everyone looked at me—the annoying person, sitting there wanting something. A waiter came over, and he wasn't happy—I could tell by his body language. He picked up the coffee pot *that had been sitting on my table all along* and poured me some coffee. I tried to explain scotomas to him, but he was gone in a moment.

Isn't it amazing how the mind works? I had told myself that the only way to get some coffee was to ask a waiter. As soon as I did that, I developed a scotoma to the pot sitting on my table. I had noticed the salt and pepper shakers, which were dwarfed by the coffeepot. I looked around the room, and sure enough, every single table in the restaurant had a coffeepot. Why hadn't I seen it before? Scotoma.

O.O.P.S.™

O.O.P.S.™ (Original Opening Premise Scotoma) is a very powerful acronym that will accelerate your growth in direct proportion to your ability to be conscious of it. I "oopsed" the coffeepot. I told myself that coffee comes from waiters, and because of that I developed a scotoma. It was my *limiting* Original Opening Premise that created that Scotoma. Once I believed my opening premise, the scotoma was the offspring of my idea. You can eliminate many scotomas from occurring by paying close attention to your original opening premise—your OOPS. Here are some examples of the OOPS concept at work:

- I can't find my keys.
- I don't remember her name.
- I can't seem to make enough money.
- Getting in shape has always been difficult for me.
- I guess I should stop complaining. It will never get any better.

All of the above statements create scotomas. Without you even being aware of it, these limiting statements turn your brain off. The next time you wonder why life's not flowing the way you would like it to, ask yourself what you've been thinking about. I'll bet you'll discover your own OOPS.

A Final Note

Everything you need to be successful in your life is right in front of you *right now*. If you think that it's somewhere else, you'll build a scotoma to it. *Your scotomas are limiting beliefs that you have about yourself or other people.*

Ninety-five percent of your reality is based on what you see. At the same time, science has discovered that based on the information available to the human eye, we are able to pick up less than one trillionth of the information that's available. One trillionth. We make up 95 percent of our reality based on one trillionth of the information that is available to us. If you could only improve your perception by one 0.001 of one percent, you would be light years ahead of everyone else.

The reality is that we are all in this thing called life together. We all have more neurons than we could ever hope to use in our lifetime, and certainly more than enough to get exactly what we want out of life. In fact, that's what you and I are getting out of life *right now*—exactly what we expect. When you learn how to change your expectations, you will absolutely transform your life. We all have limited perception. What if it was possible to break through those scotomas? What would life be presenting to us? Let's find out!

Lesson 1
Reflection Questions

Behavior follows attitude. Can you think of a time in your life when a negative attitude led to a poor result? Jot it down.

_____

_____

_____

_____

_____

_____

Next, think of a time when you've locked on to a positive attitude about a person, an event, etc. What negative elements did you overlook because you were locked on to the positive?

_____

_____

_____

_____

_____

What one aspect of your life could you now apply this "lock on" concept to, with positive results?

Think of a thing or person you've developed a scotoma about. How does this cause you to act? What can you do to change this?

Explain the OOPS formula. Make note of a few of your own OOPS and then ask yourself how you will benefit when you change your original opening premises.

I take away the following from this lesson …

I intend to use it first in the areas of …

Because …

List the behaviors you would like to change, or visions you would like to accomplish:

Lesson 2: Dial 1-800-RAS for Success

*" Man's capacities have never been measured;
nor are we able to judge of what he can do
by any precedents, so little has been tried."*
— Henry David Thoreau (1817–1862)

As I stated at the end of the first lesson, once you change your perceptions and expectations, you will change your life. How does this happen? You will have a new *vision* about what your life can become, and this new vision will trigger a powerful force within yourself. You'll "see" new opportunities, you'll be able to overcome virtually any obstacle, and your life will be transformed by the changes that take place within and around you.

A Key to Prosperity: RAS

So what is this "powerful force" used to overcome any obstacle, and how do I obtain it? I've got good news for you: you already possess this "incredible tool." It's called the Reticular Activating System (RAS). The RAS is about as big as your pinky and connects your brain to your spinal cord.

What does the RAS do? It is an alerting device that keeps us conscious. If your RAS is damaged, you'll slip into a coma. If it's damaged permanently, you'll never waken again. Your heart may continue beating and all of your organs may continue to function, but you will never awaken into this thing called life again. It's that important.

This net-like group of cells at the base of the brain also performs another important function. It screens out unnecessary information that's of absolutely no use in getting what you want. Think of the RAS as a good executive assistant. The company president doesn't open all the mail and take all the calls. Somebody screens the mail and the messages, *letting only the most important information get through*.

That's the key to the RAS: *it only lets the information through to your brain that you perceive is important*.

We're bombarded daily with sights, sounds, images and so on. The RAS screens out most of it. Why? Well, for one thing, there's too much information out there. Imagine you're on a long driving trip. You're going hundreds of miles. Do you "see" every exit that you pass by? Every billboard? No. But what happens when you know that you're getting close to where you want to go? Suddenly all the exit signs and billboards become much more important.

Because it filters information, the RAS can be your best friend or your worst enemy. What if you woke up with a bad attitude and thought that your entire day was going to be a series of inconveniences and negative experiences? Guess what? The RAS would only allow the information and images that support your beliefs to reach your brain and not knowing what's going on, you believe you're right because that's all the information you can see.

But the opposite is also true. What if you'd awakened this morning and said to yourself, "Man, this is going to be a *great* day! I'm going to have fun with my family, make progress on my visions, and enjoy myself to the fullest!" What do you think that would do to your RAS? It would open it to everything that matches your original premise.

The RAS is the key to prosperity, to living the life that you've always dreamed about.

> When you become aware of how the RAS works and use it as this book outlines, you will be able to accomplish more in the next year than you have in the last five, and you won't have to work any harder.

That's a heck of a proclamation, isn't it? That's the great thing about the RAS: you don't have to work harder or smarter. You simply have to program your RAS to let in what you want (we'll get to *how* you do this in a moment, but know it will focus on your vision), and all the information you need will come to you.

Threat vs. Value

Let's spend a few more minutes understanding the RAS. People consciously or unconsciously program their RAS to let two types of information—also called motivators—reach their brain:

1. Information they perceive as a ***threat***

2. Information they perceive as having ***value***

By far the most common type of motivator is a *threat*. It's still the most readily used motivator today, both in the corporate world and even in families. (By the way, it's the *worst* motivator you can use if you're interested in achieving accelerated, long-term performance and living longer.) Why is this the case? Simple: threats get our attention because *we are afraid we are going to lose something important to us—maybe even our lives*. Most of us have been conditioned this way our whole lives. If you're sitting in a movie theater and someone rushes in and yells "Fire!" you'll pay attention. Not too many people say, "How do you know for sure?" Instead, you'll take immediate action, especially if the person shouting "Fire!" sounds serious.

Threat is a militaristic approach to motivating someone: "When I want your opinion, I'll give it to you." It has its place in certain situations, and the military is a good example. Soldiers must follow orders. When a sergeant wants her squad to take a hill, she doesn't want her soldiers questioning the order. There's no place for comments like, "Oh, I don't know if I want to take *that* hill. That hill's dangerous. Is there another hill we can take?" In this case, you don't want people thinking for themselves. Others could get hurt. It's the same situation if someone yells "Fire!" in a crowded movie theater. The goal is to get out.

As effective as threat can be as a motivator, both inwardly ("If I don't lose weight, I'll die") and outwardly ("If you don't get that assignment in on time, I'll make you stay late until you get it right and humiliate you in front of your peers"), it limits long-term performance. When threatened, people will only do enough to eliminate the threat. Working under a threat means working under a great deal of stress, which is devastating to the body. *Many studies have shown that there is little, if any, value in using threat as a motivator.*

The second form of motivation—the type of motivation this book is all about—is *value*. Both threat and value are incredible motivators. While threat simply motivates a person to do just enough to get by, value brings out the best in a person and others around her. Value is all about having choices and making decisions. To put this another way, value is the music that makes your life rock.

So what does this have to do with the RAS? Here's how the RAS works: have you ever bought a car, and then, while driving home from the dealership, noticed several other cars almost exactly like yours (or at least the same model)? Why do you see these cars now, when you never would have noticed them before? You've opened up your awareness to a particular "thing"—in this case, a particular make and model of a car. This make and model of car now has value to you, and because of this value, your RAS allows you to "see" the information.

Here's an important point to remember:

> Determine what is significant, and you
> will see it everywhere.

The value-threat motivators also work when you're sleeping. Think of a mother sleeping soundly in her bed. Her preteen daughter is having a sleepover downstairs, and the girls are making plenty of noise and playing music. A train rattles by on nearby tracks, shaking the house. Dad's watching TV right next to her, but still. Mom sleeps. Suddenly, two doors down, the family's three-month-old baby lets out a whimper. Mom immediately wakes up. In seconds, she's wide awake and tending the child.

Why didn't the giggling of the girls wake up Mom? What about the father watching TV, or the train rattling by? They didn't wake her because they didn't pose a threat or value to her family. But when the baby cried out, Mom woke up. She heard the cry and considered it a threat or value, and her RAS let that information into her brain.

Do you see why the RAS is so important? The only information that gets by it is what you have predetermined to be significant. Nothing else gets past our executive secretaries. We develop scotomas for everything we don't perceive as a threat or consider to have value.

We can also create imaginary threats. Consider the family again: night after night, Dad sleeps soundly. One weekend, his wife takes the children on a short trip to see family. The first night, he's alone. As he lies in bed, he begins to hear strange noises. Suddenly things are different. Why? *Because now his RAS is letting in new information, even information he's manufactured in his own mind.*

Significance vs. Observations

What have you determined to be significant? If it's significant to you that you don't get along with a certain person, what kind of information will your RAS allow to reach your brain? You'll allow any information that supports why you don't like the person. In fact, you'll build scotomas to help you believe what you think you believe. You'll be rude to the person. You might not listen to him. You might turn away. You might not make eye contact with him. As you can see, what you determine to be significant can limit you. How? You already know what's going to happen. In other words, you let in the information that conforms with your preconditioned attitude, and then you act accordingly. OOPS. What you determine to be significant gets right to the core of your vision.

Let me tell you another story. One day I was out shopping with my daughter Courtney for shoes. I had recently started my own business, so I was moving a million miles a minute. I wanted to get the shoes quickly and get out of the mall.

On our way to the shoe store, we hurried by a bookstore. All of a sudden, out of the corner of my eye, I noticed a book in the window. We screeched to a halt. The book's title was something like, *How to Succeed in Business Your First Time Out*. I ran into the store and picked up a copy, expecting it to be dedicated to me and printed that very day. To my surprise, the book had first been printed twenty years before!

Why hadn't I ever noticed that book? Starting my own business hadn't been a significant part of my life before, so my RAS screened out anything having to do with starting and succeeding in a business. Why don't you grab the ketchup when you are looking for an apple? Do you see how powerful the RAS can be? at the same time, you don't have to worry about over-extending your RAS. At any given time, your RAS can categorize thousands of things as "significant." This is far more than you'll need to accomplish your visions.

Here's another example: you're sitting at home watching TV, and suddenly the set blows up! Poof! It's history. You pick up your local newspaper and right there on page eight is a full-page ad for televisions—20 percent off. You think, "It's my lucky day!" Is it really luck? No! There's no such thing as luck. Luck is simply the outcome of opportunity meeting preparedness.

What do you see on the way to purchase the television? Billboards advertising televisions. Once you determine what you are looking for, the information is suddenly available. Remember what "high performers" know: *the vision comes first, and then I see; I do not see first.* You may have read the entire newspaper before the television blew up, but chances are you wouldn't have noticed the sale on television sets.

Everything you need to be successful is right in front of you, *right now*, but until you decide what you're looking for, you won't see it. I know it sounds simple—maybe too simple. The more you learn about how incredible you are, the more you'll see how easy it is to get what you want. *Stop paying so much attention to what you've become, and start paying attention to who you truly are.*

How do you take advantage of your RAS?

On a recent evening, I decided to kick back and watch some TV. I turned on a show that bored me and didn't make me feel very good about myself. All in all, I knew I'd be much happier watching something else. As I was talking to myself about how I wished I could be watching a different channel, I clicked the "info" button and got even worse news—this boring show would be on for another hour. An hour of discomfort. I was so disappointed. This wasn't at all what I wanted to happen. I continued to watch, but the time just crawled by. Why did this have to happen to me? I spend a fortune each month for satellite television, and there I was, watching something I didn't like. It's wasn't fair!

What have you been thinking about as I've shared my sorrows with you? Perhaps you thought that I seem a little thick in the head. "Why the heck doesn't he just change the channel? What does he think the remote is for? Why would anyone sit through something he doesn't like?"

When you're in a situation you don't like, why don't you change the channel? For instance, what about these situations:

- I don't like the shape I'm in …
- I don't like my job …
- I'm not getting paid enough …
- My spouse doesn't treat me right …
- My parents don't understand me …
- I'm not tall enough …
- I'm not attractive …
- I don't have enough hair …
- I'm not smart enough …
- I'm too smart …
- Everyone around me is incompetent …
- No one seems to know me for who I really am …

Have you ever found yourself watching that station in your life? And you think I'm thick?

Do you know why you find yourself watching those stations, even though it's not what you want? You probably never realized that your brain has its own remote control. Your RAS is your remote. If the RAS is your remote, how do you use it to change the channel? It's easy. *Since the current channel you're watching is a result of the thoughts you're thinking, not the behavior you're experiencing, simply take a mental "time-out," grab your remote, and change the channel by changing your thinking.* How do I do this? Simple. Ask yourself this incredibly simple, yet powerful question: "How do I want it to be?"

This is a very powerful question—so powerful that it bears repeating: how can you change your thinking, and hence your resulting behavior? Ask yourself either of these questions:

> How do I want it to be, or do I want to be?

Here's an important point to remember: an unacceptable answer to this question is: "I don't know... anyone would feel this way if they were in this situation."

First, you are not just anyone. Second, don't just fire up the same old neurons. Fire up *new* ones if you want different results. Let's remind ourselves again of what Einstein said: "We can't solve problems by using the same thinking we used when we created them." By asking, "How do I want it to be?" you are opening your RAS to new information and possibilities, resulting in a new perspective and a changed channel.

If you are dissatisfied with your weight, for example, you must ask yourself what weight you want to reach. Then you can consider how you'll receive value from that weight rather than focusing on "how" you're going to accomplish reaching that weight. We'll discuss the "how" in much more detail later, but for now, just recognize that focusing on how you are going to obtain your visions is the worst thing you want to think about when creating new visions. (I'll get into when the "how" is important in more detail in Lesson 6.)

No matter what it is, if a situation is not allowing you to have the time of your life *right now*, by asking "How do I want it to be?" your creative mind will begin to provide solutions to the new vision, which then creates new behaviors. At that point, you've "changed your channel" and, ultimately, your attitude. Remember, attitude has a one hundred percent effect on your behavior and life.

How Do I Want It to Be?

If you're like most people, right about now you're probably thinking, "Okay, Larry, I get the RAS. I understand what it does. But *how* am I going to achieve the visions and dreams that I have?"

You'll have to be more patient. As I mentioned a moment ago, right now is the worst time in the world to identify "how" you're going to succeed, because you don't have a handle on the vision yet. (The same thing applies to teams: never introduce the "how" until everyone's convinced they want the vision. If you want to find out all the reasons why something can't be done, introduce the "how" too soon. Otherwise, you're finding the perfect way to get to Seattle with a group that wants to be in Miami.)

What visions do you have of yourself? What is your RAS open to? If I see myself as a lean, keen, change-agent machine with sweat dripping off my pecs and my washboard stomach, what happens when I walk by a tray of muffins? I love muffins! I'd love to gobble one or two. And I will…if I don't have a new vision. Because of the power behind a vision, I can easily walk by a plate of muffins because they have nothing to do with my vision. They are not significant. I build a scotoma to them. Without the new vision I'm stuck with the old one, and the old vision will surely gobble up those muffins.

Visions provide direction to our thoughts and actions. What if, when I saw that tray of muffins, I thought, "Well, you know, I can always work out tomorrow, and those muffins look pretty darn good. Besides, they're free. In fact, I better take two in case I miss lunch." If I take those muffins, I'll think, "You're so weak—here you go again! What'd you expect? I've tried to be a lean, keen, change-agent machine, but nothing seems to work."

Am I not capable of becoming a lean, keen, change-agent machine? No. It's not working because I lack a new vision. When this happens, we're motivated by nothing more than a threat. How many people want to get in shape so that they won't die prematurely? How many people want to do a good job at work so they won't get fired? That's being motivated by threats, not value. You must first decide why you want something—what's in it for you—and then you must also stifle the urge to dwell on *how* you'll achieve it. The "how" is essential, but there's a time and a place for it, as we'll learn shortly.

The key to developing a vision is to ask yourself this question: "How do I want my life to be?" This all starts in your mind. You use old neurons to perpetuate a situation. *To change your thinking and thus change your attitude, you must fire new neurons to create a new sense of who you are and what you are capable of doing or becoming.*

How do you want it to be? The human brain is an awesome thing! When you ask, "How do I want it to be?" you fire new neurons. You're on your way to setting a vision, which influences your thinking, which influences your attitude, which influences your behavior.

But what happens to the person who says, "I don't know how I want my life to be?" Everyone knows people like this.

"What do you want to be when you grow up?"

"I don't know."

"What do you want to study in college?"

"I'm not sure."

"What kind of career do you want to have?"

"I don't know."

If you've ever felt this way yourself, what usually happens? You'll find somebody else who feels that same way, too, because misery loves company. And then you're really stuck, aren't you?

When you ask, "How do I want my life to be?" and create a new vision, you leave the current situation behind and create a new situation. All you have to do is change the remote inside your head. The same thing applies with people and relationships, too.

"I don't like her!"

"Why not?"

"She annoys me to no end!"

Wait a minute—how do I want it to be? *I'm comfortable with who I am. I share my ideas with others, but they don't have to agree with me. They are who they are, and I like being around people, even though I don't necessarily agree with all of them.*

All of a sudden, I'm calm and relaxed. If I'm interacting with a person I don't like in this new, calm way, what'll happen? She will pick up on it immediately, and her thinking and behavior may change as well. Here's a key point to remember:

> Negative emotions about yourself, a situation, or another person are simply a symptom of not having a positive vision of what you want in that area.

Here's something else to know: you have to not only *want* the change, you have to *own* it, and by that I mean that your thoughts, attitudes, and behaviors must all be in sync. You can't simply "try." The road to failure is littered with people who are *trying* to succeed. Why? Because "trying" introduces an element of doubt into your thinking. Your subconscious mind, which can't differentiate between an actual event and one that you have imagined, picks up on this. Doubt leads to hesitation, and hesitation leads to failure.

Vision Must Come First

High-performance people know that vision comes first, before they can "see." They do not see what they need to see first. If you look at what's available first—in terms of aptitudes, talents, or resources—your visions will be limited to what you can see. When you establish the vision first, however, your RAS dials in the information necessary for you to accomplish the vision. If you haven't identified what you want, your RAS doesn't know what information to allow in to your brain. It will only let in what matches your current perception of yourself and others.

Without a vision, life is happening *to* you. With a vision, you are happening to life. Trust me: there's a *huge* difference between those two statements.

You have to see yourself "win" first before you can succeed. When I first began my company, Aperneo, I knew nothing about running a business. I asked many people for advice, and most of them told me, "Don't go into business for yourself!" There's a frequently quoted statistic that 85 percent of all businesses fail in their first year. Instead, I chose a different attitude. I decided that I was going to be one of the 15 percent who succeeded. This was very new: earlier in my life, I would have been focused on nothing but that 85 percent failure rate. But the more I began to apply these principles, the faster the transformation occurred.

When I took my daughter to the mall that day, we were there to buy shoes, and that's what we were focused on. Because I had a vision about starting my own business, my RAS was open to that type of information, and as a result, I "saw" that book. Did I have to work any harder to find the book? Nope. Once your brain knows what you want, you don't have to work hard to get it.

When you learn the L.I.F.E. lessons, you will understand how to accomplish vision instead of just accomplishing goals. Goal accomplishment is like cramming for a test. You memorize a block of information, screening out everything else, and then immediately after the test you forget it all and move on to the next test.

You might be thinking, "But what if I create a vision and then fail?" Or, "I've tried to follow a vision before, but it didn't work out."

If you fail, you must simply try again. The average person will fail three times before giving up. Thomas Edison failed over 10,000 times before successfully inventing the light bulb. Why didn't he quit? Because he knew he would ultimately succeed. He had a vision. We must first believe, and then we will see.

Here's another point about failure: if you fail at something, don't think that you're a failure. You're not. You simply tried something, and it didn't work. But now you know that the particular thing you tried doesn't work. Remember, you're a genius—you have billions of neurons that can be fired at will. You haven't failed; what hasn't worked has been nothing more than an idea, a hypothesis, or a plan.

Don't give up attempting to make your vision a reality. Any time you give up, your neurons party. Why? They don't have to work; they aren't challenged. Things normally move toward inaction. Avoid the trap of trying something once, and stopping right there if the results aren't *exactly* what you wanted. With a strong vision, you will carry through to the end, no matter how many hardships and failures you endure along the way.

A Final Note

Your successes begin with a clear vision. The key is to create this vision out of a sense of want and a sense of value. Remember, threat is driven by "I have to." You've been conditioned to respond to threats. You haven't usually been conditioned to create and respond to a vision.

Who makes the decision about what to respond to? You do.

That's what's so essential about what you're learning. You're learning much more than how to smell the flowers along the way—some people have allergies, after all. Instead, you're learning to be present, to live in the moment. If you're not having the time of your life *right now*, then you don't have a vision.

> If I don't get a new vision, I'm destined to live the old one.

This can be so powerful. Every moment can be magical. The next time you take a shower, really *feel* the water on your skin. That's a different concept, isn't it? How many times have you been in the shower without the slightest awareness that you were in the shower? You're thinking, "I'd better hurry, gotta get going, gotta hurry up!" You rush out of the shower, rush into your clothes, and rush off to work. Later, you rush home, and what's happened? You've rushed from one thing to another all day. You're wound up and filled with stress. Your kids want to play with you, but you're too tired to do anything.

Having a vision will help you live in the moment. You'll feel the water in the shower, you'll rediscover your children, you'll fall in love with your spouse all over again, and you'll remember how unique and special you really are.

Everything begins with a vision.

Lesson 2
Reflection Questions

What is it about others that draws you to them?

What first impressions have you created that you need to tweak or change to improve your relationships with others?

What scotomas have you developed that have held you back from achieving or becoming what you want?

How can you use the RAS to fulfill your visions?

List at least three areas in your life where "changing the channel" would improve the quality of the very precious and special life that you have.

Explain in writing why the vision comes first and then you see, and you do not see first.

I take away the following insight from this lesson ...

I intend to use it first in the areas of ...

_____
_____
_____
_____
_____

Because ...

_____
_____
_____
_____

List the behaviors you would like to change or visions you would like to accomplish:

_____
_____
_____
_____
_____
_____
_____
_____
_____
_____
_____
_____

Lesson 3: How Successful Can You Be Driving Into the Future, Looking Through the Rear-View Mirror?

"Men feel disturbed not by things, but by the views they take of them." — Epictus, 1st century

In this lesson, we'll move beyond the RAS and the concepts of lock on/lock out. Next, we'll uncover what happens inside your brain during the split second when a thought is transformed into a behavior. This is one of the most powerful components of the L.I.F.E. lessons: The more clearly you understand how your brain works, the easier it will be to understand your own thinking. Having this new understanding will enable you to take constructive action when things don't go the way you want them to. You will be able to talk yourself into what you want, rather than talking yourself out of getting what you want. The brain must operate on a trial-and-error process if it lacks a vision. It will just try and fail, try and fail, and try and fail, *ad infinitum*, until it gets a pretty good sense of what works and what doesn't.

Remember how closely thinking and behavior are linked. Thoughts determine attitudes, which in turn determine behavior. The more you understand how your brain works, the more you can influence your own thinking and consequently change your behaviors. The mind is so powerful that you won't have to consciously attempt to manipulate behavior for desired results; instead, it will happen automatically.

As we learn, so we become. It doesn't take much learning, either. Think about a child. By the time most children are about eight years old, they will hear the word "no" an average of 100,000 times, but they will only hear "yes" about 20,000 times. So when we become adults, we must teach ourselves and others to overcome all the "nos" we've heard throughout our lives. What do you say most often to yourself—yes, or no?

What you'll learn next is how the brain makes decisions. I'll describe it in a somewhat simplistic fashion, even though the actual thinking process is extremely complex. While you are reading the next few pages, you will find that the purpose for learning how we make decisions is to correct thought processes when things don't go the way we want them to go instead of allowing evidence to change our visions.

What Your Truth Is, and How the "Cup" Made It So

Imagine that you are very young and don't know whether you can pick up a cup or not. You have never tried before, so neurologically you have no experience and no idea yet of what kind of a cup picker-upper you are.

Your mother asks you to pick up the cup. The first time you try, it tips over. She asks you to try again, and it tips over again. What's happening? Your brain is recording the evidence of your attempts, and so far you are falling short of succeeding.

Being the tenacious individual you are, you continue to try. On the next attempt, you tip it over again, and everyone who is watching begins to laugh at your behavior. Their laughter is also recorded by your brain—never to be lost, never to be forgotten. The emotion of what you are experiencing is also being recorded. Enough is enough. In your frustration, you accept that the evidence regarding your ability to pick up the cup must be the truth, so you quit. The results of what just happened have produced not only an attitude, but a belief about your expertise at picking up a cup.

This same process has taken place in many, many areas of your life. Through this process, you discover what kind of speller, athlete, artist, mathematician, typist, friend, lover, and spouse you are. If you were successful at picking up the cup, then you have a positive belief; if you weren't, then you have a negative one. So what can we learn from this?

Edison and the Power of Vision

Thomas Edison's many attempts to create a light bulb reveal a very powerful truth. As I mentioned earlier, by his own admission Edison "tipped the cup over," if you will, more than 10,000 times before the light went on. Since the average individual quits after three failures, what created so much endurance and tenacity in Edison? When Edison looked at the evidence—his failures—instead of thinking, "I don't work," he thought, "these attempts didn't work," and continued until the evidence matched his vision, rather than the evidence creating the vision. The powerful truth that Edison's example teaches us is this:

> You must believe first and let the evidence appear, rather than letting the evidence determine what belief will appear.

That is what this book is all about. Determine *first* what you want, and then don't stop until the evidence supports your belief. The more we know about how we think and how thinking affects behavior, the more prosperous we will become. Let's find out more about the power of our own thinking.

The Thought Process

I'd like you to mentally go back in time to when you were totally immersed in liquid, inside your mother's womb. While you were developing in the womb, your brain was forming at a phenomenally rapid rate—so rapid, in fact, that it was consuming 85 percent of your carbohydrates and protein. The brain formed rapidly because it serves, if you will, as the headquarters (no pun intended) to everything that is physiologically you. At the same time, you were also learning things that were so essential to life that nature couldn't take the chance on you having to learn these things on your own.

What are some of these processes? After you ate your last meal, did you have to consciously think about how to extract the protein from the food, break it down, and send it through your system? No, because your digestive systems were programmed before you were born. Think about all the things your body does automatically— producing and circulating your blood, for example. Do you consciously think, "Hey, there's a viral infection in the room. I should increase my white cell count now." Breathing is another thing programmed prior to birth. At this moment, are you inhaling or exhaling? Here's another one. You're at a barbecue chatting with a friend, and you accidentally rest your hand on the scorching hot barbecue's surface. What happens? Do you continue your conversation, suddenly notice an awful smell, and *then* pull your hand away? No, it doesn't work that way. You pull your hand away immediately, because you are pre-wired to not inflict damage on yourself. These systems are programmed for one reason only—survival. Our physiology was pre-programmed at birth.

What about all the other thinking that we do after we're born? Our genetic makeup plays a major role in who we are, but it plays a much smaller role in what we become—in the opinions of some, as little as 20 percent. It contributes the pre-programmed aspects of who we are, why we look the way we look, the gifts that we have, as well as our temperament.

But what about the other 80 percent? The majority of what we become is determined by what we think about. *It's not so much the experiences we've had, but more importantly how we talked to ourselves about those experiences.* In other words, it's our thinking—the *thought process.*

Even though your thought process was programmed at birth, what you choose to think about was not. Be sure you highlight this next sentence, because it is the why behind how you currently see yourself in all areas of your life. *You've learned who you are not by what has happened to you, but how you've talked to yourself about what has happened to you.*

Since you and I were born successful, with amazing brains, why aren't we successful in all areas of our lives? Because we've been programmed *not* to be. Remember all those "nos" we've heard all our lives? Others have determined most of our thinking: parents, siblings, teachers, people in our community, and so on.

Remember, it's not *what* you think, but *how* you think that's all-important. And that gets to the heart of Lesson 3.

The Subconscious

Let's learn more about how the brain functions. Below consciousness lies the *subconscious.* The subconscious stores information; in fact, it has been doing so since the moment you were born. (It has also been storing information prior to birth, but we don't need to get into that here.)

Almost everything that has ever happened to you is stored permanently in your subconscious. In fact, your subconscious has not only stored what happened, but also how you talked to yourself about each occurrence. (Think of it this way: You've stored not only the actual size of the fish you caught, but also how big you told everyone the fish was. The fish that ends up becoming real to you is the one you thought and talked about.) You also stored how you felt about each event—in other words, all of the emotions tied to each event. Scientists have discovered that memories of emotions do not diminish over time. So no matter what the situation, more often than not it will cause you to feel a certain way, even though the feeling was *not* necessarily created at that moment in time.

Why is this important? If you are to bring out the best in yourself, you must overcome what has already been stored in your subconscious to change your thinking and subsequently change your behavior. In Lesson 1, I gave an example about asking you to sing in front of a group of your peers. Every thing that ever happened to you in your life regarding singing—both positive and negative—was stirred up in your subconscious when I said, "In a moment, you're going to sing a song."

A high school counselor once told me, "Don't go to college." He thought I had no focus, but I interpreted his comment to mean that I wasn't smart enough for college, despite having good grades. It has been a long time since he told me that, but do I still remember it? Occasionally I remember it consciously, but my subconscious remembers it almost every time a related instance occurs. Every time I find myself in a place where my mental abilities are challenged, what's one of the things my subconscious remembers. *Don't go to college.* OOPS. This sort of negative thinking continues in all of us until we decide to create a new subconscious picture that replaces the limiting one.

Information stored in the subconscious is called the *truth*. But what really is a truth in life? It's nothing more than our *perception* of the truth, isn't it? This is what we label "truth," or, to use another term, reality. If you're interested in growing beyond what you've become, you must understand this point: The person reading this information knows more about who he has become, rather than who he is. Let's use the "iceberg analogy"—what you've become is only the tip of the iceberg, and who you are, and what you are capable of, is the rest of the iceberg that lies below the water's surface.

Is your truth about yourself the lid on your potential, or is it the stuff that visions are made of and manifested from? *The truth is that you and I have not even scratched the surface of what is possible for us!*

To begin the transformation of becoming what you have always dreamed of being, you must realize that the life that you lead is the result of your decisions. To transform your current reality, you must understand how your decisions are made subconsciously, so you can consciously alter the process and automatically change behavior to achieve the results you desire.

Vision accomplishment is a natural result of the decisions you make relative to your new vision, not the result of decisions you have already made. How can you drive into the future while you are looking in the rear-view mirror?

Four Steps to Making Decisions

A key reason for learning more about how the brain operates is the decision-making process. Your decisions have created the life you are currently living. Everything that has happened to you, as well as what you have created for yourself, is a result of your thinking.

Think back to when I told you to sing a song in front of a group. What happened? The song became a stimulus. Then what happened? Your brain searched for similar past experiences, and you responded with an old attitude.

But how did all that take place? What happened to cause you to prepare yourself to either be successful or experience something you'd attempt to avoid?

Here's a simple, yet scientific approach to how you make a decision:

1. We receive information through our own perceptions. This happens via our senses (taste, touch, sight, smell, and hearing).

2. Our minds analyze the information and then search for associations. The mind asks itself, "Have I seen, heard, smelled, felt, or tasted anything like this before?"

3. Our minds make an evaluation based on existing information. Evaluated items fall into two main categories: Will this be *good* for me, or will this be *bad* for me?

4. We make a decision about what to do, say, or think. This decision usually involves the fight-or-flight mechanism. We tend to either push back or avoid completely any situation or stimulus we perceive as negative. In the case of a positive past experience, we move toward what we perceive as having value.

These four steps normally happen in the snap of a finger. As discussed earlier, you may not even realize that you've already made up your mind about your thinking and subsequent behavior. This happens many times during the day. How does the fight-or-flight mechanism come into play? We fight by finding fault with ourselves or others. "Sing a song? What a stupid exercise." We flee by trying to become invisible. "If he doesn't see me, he won't call on me to sing the song." If we have an opportunity to leave altogether, we will; if not, we'll stay but won't allow ourselves to get anything positive out of the experience.

The Power of Sanity in Self-Image

We discussed earlier that the primary function of the subconscious is to store information. One of the systems of the subconscious is the *creative subconscious*. Its job is to maintain your sanity and remind you that you're "right," no matter what the circumstances. This is the main reason why we'd rather be right than successful, even though intellectually, most of us would like to be successful *and* right.

So let's ask an all-important question: What is sanity? *Sanity is the self-image that is currently dominant.* It's how we see ourselves now in every area of our lives. This currently dominant self-image isn't about how we once were, and it's not about how we could be. It's how we see ourselves right now. What's more, you and I are wired to make certain that we are right, no matter what. Otherwise, something would be "wrong" with us, and we can't have that, can we?

Are you ready for two more earth-shattering questions? *Whose is the only sanity that you can maintain? Whose sanity are you scientifically, as well as physiologically, wired to maintain?* No one's except your own, of course. Why is this so important?

> You are in no danger of ever changing another human being.

If you have been attempting to change someone other than yourself, you need to stop immediately. When you attempt to change another person, you are saying that their current behavior is unacceptable. Perhaps you think that the other person will suddenly come up to you, give you a big hug, and say, "You know, you're right. I should change. This is going to make me a better person. Thanks." No way. It's human nature to push back and resist change. Change is the second greatest fear humans possess, and no matter how low a person's self-esteem may be, he or she will still retain enough dignity to resist being pushed around. No one likes being told what to do.

This works with feelings, too. How often do parents tell their children, "You shouldn't feel that way?" Doing so does nothing less than tell the child that not even his or her feelings are "correct." Instead, the parent could say, "I can see that really hurts. How are you feeling right now? Do you want to keep feeling that way?" Once the child got past the shock of this response and truly believed that the parent was sincere, the child would open up and move past the problem. Expressing feelings, having them acknowledged, and then being counseled about how to begin thinking about how you want to feel—that's true comfort. We'll all go out of our way for someone who listens to and encourages us.

The third element of making a decision is the point when the mind makes an evaluation based on existing information. Where does this existing information come from? It comes from thoughts and past experiences. When you see or hear something, your brain immediately attempts to evaluate it based on your past experiences. Consider a man who's just gone through a terrible divorce. All of a sudden, he's created a global attitude about all women based on just one—his former wife. Later, he might meet an incredible woman—someone truly exceptional inside and out—and think, "Have I ever seen anything like this before? What is this possibly leading me toward?" If he does, he will find fault with this wonderful person before he's even given himself the opportunity to fully get to know her. OOPS.

If we can't change others, who's the only person we can change? Ourselves, right? I learned this the hard way. I often found fault with others instead of myself. Here's an example of what I mean: 25 years ago, a buddy and I compared notes to see who'd had the most jobs. I won, but only by one—I'd had 23. These weren't all short-term jobs, either. I spent six years as a teacher and almost three years as a contractor. I was a musician. I cut hair for a while; that didn't work out because everyone got the same haircut. I sold life insurance for two and a half years. I was the general manager for a multifranchise automobile dealership for almost three years. The list goes on and on.

What happened each and every time? I'd reach a point in my career where I wasn't being respected, wasn't being treated right, and wasn't being paid enough money. I reacted just as you might think I would—I found another job. It never took long before I wasn't being respected, wasn't being treated right, and wasn't being paid enough at *that* job, so I'd go find *another* job. I kept moving from job to job, from career to career, because someone or something was always wrong. The problem was never me, of course—I had to be right.

Eventually, I learned a very important lesson: *Until you learn how to change your mind, you'll have to change your job, your spouse, and everything else.*

Here's another thing I learned from having all these different jobs and careers—*what* we do isn't important. Whether you're a brain surgeon or a custodian, it makes no difference; it's *how you feel* about what you're doing that makes all the difference. Quite frankly, it doesn't matter to anyone else what you're doing, either; it's *how you deliver* what you're doing to somebody else that creates the only difference worth remembering.

Incredible things can happen when you change yourself and don't attempt to change others. During my time in the car business, I became the general manager of a large dealership. On my first day at work, three people quit—the three people who thought they should have been named general manager.

My training program before I became general manager taught me about the importance of having a clear vision that is shared by all, not dictated by one.

In the first month of training, I worked behind the parts counter and heard all day about what a bunch of uncaring, "I-want-it-now" people the service technicians were. The sales staff were all prima donnas, by the way, because they always wanted everything right now too!

My next stint was with the technicians, who filled me in on what a bunch of jerks the parts people were. How dare they spend more time with the customers than with the technicians—didn't they see who their biggest customers really were? To the technicians, the parts people worried much more about obsolescence than about having the parts on hand when they were needed. They also thought the sales people were a bunch of prima donnas.

After that, I became a salesman and learned that the salespeople's feelings about the people in parts and service were no different.

It was clear to me: Each department had its own vision. The dealership was in disarray as a result. I knew very little at the time about the car business, but I knew a great deal about people. I met with the managers of each department and made a point of telling them that it didn't get any better than who they were. I also confided in them that my only role was to create an environment where they could succeed, and that they had to let me know what they needed to be successful.

In turn, they quickly learned that no one person or department was any better or more important than the other team members. I told them that as long as they always put others first, we would all enjoy rewards far beyond what they were capable of doing alone. None of them wanted to let me down, so each person performed like he or she was the best. In the first year, we exceeded our profit goals and received the President's Award for dealership excellence and exceptional customer satisfaction.

Remember: I knew nothing about the car business. But I knew what people wanted. I didn't try to change them. Instead, I helped them set a vision in their minds and let them change themselves. The results were and are inevitable: prosperity.

The Power of Self-Image

As I just mentioned, I once was in the auto business, and today I have quite a few clients who are in the business as well. I think we all know that car salespeople get a pretty bad rap from the public, don't they? Of course, there are many less-than-reputable auto salesmen that do a pretty good job of perpetuating a negative image by flagrantly exhibiting a lack of integrity and values. The perception is usually of someone pretty sleazy—he might be wearing white loafers and gold chains; he's a liar; he's going to trick you if he can. Unfortunately, many people who sell cars buy into this image, too. If they're asked by someone they don't know what they do for a living, they'll probably reply in a very low voice, "I, uh, I sell cars."

"You what?"

Again, a muffled response: "I sell cars."

Folks who feel this way feel that what they do determines how they feel about themselves.

At the same time, there are plenty of other people who sell cars who don't buy into the myths of the "typical" car salesperson. If someone asks them what they do, they reply confidently, "I'm in the car business. What are you driving?" They're proud of what they do.

It doesn't matter what we do—what matters is how we *feel* about what we are doing. Let me clarify that a little: it's not even so much how we feel about what we do, it's really about how we feel about ourselves, mostly because we bring our self-image to everything we do. If you don't like how you feel about yourself in one or more areas of your life, you must change your self-image. To do so, you'll probably first try to change your behavior, and if you don't know any better, you'll to do it with willpower. To illustrate just how successful willpower is, a recent *USA Today* article reported that more than 95 percent of all diets fail. On top of that, 90 percent of dieters actually *gained* weight. Why? Usually because after losing a few pounds, dieters celebrate by returning to their old habits, and as a result they put more weight on. Did they fail because they tried to use willpower, or because they changed their self-image? People use willpower because they don't know that changing their self-image first will result in a change of behavior. Without this knowledge, they use power to overcome their own will, and usually nothing but frustration and failure follows.

It's basic human nature. We tend to gravitate toward the status quo. The status quo on a personal level is your self-image; on a global scale, it's the culture we live in. Most people would like nothing better than to get what they want, but if they think it's too difficult, they choose the path of least resistance and tell themselves that things aren't really that bad after all—yet.

During my seminars, I often perform the "push back" exercise to emphasize this point. I ask one person to hold up his or her hand, palm open, as if signaling someone to stop. I then open my palm and press against his or her hand. Once I begin to push, the other person immediately begins to push back. It's very simple, really—people don't like to get pushed around. No matter how we feel about ourselves at any given time, we have enough dignity to reject being told what to do. Pushing back is nothing more than instinct. *Until you understand this innate mechanism, you'll continue to unconsciously resist getting what you want.*

Humans will also do just about anything to avoid rejection, which damages self-esteem. As I mentioned earlier in the book, rejection is the number one fear of most people. People will go out of their way to avoid rejection, perhaps by avoiding new things or new people. When you avoid doing something because of a fear of rejection, you limit your successes and lower your self-esteem. How many things have *you* talked yourself out of? How ironic—you fear rejection because it will lower your self-esteem, but the avoidance techniques employed to avoid rejection do exactly the same thing.

Rejection comes from others, right? Consider this: in one of my many careers, I taught psychology to high-school seniors. On one particularly beautiful spring day, my students' hormones were going wild, and I found it nearly impossible to hold their attention. I thought, "Wow, what do I need to do get them to stay here mentally?"

Suddenly, I said, "Today we're going to talk about *rejection*." As soon as the words were out of my mouth, a girl in the class burst into tears. (One can only imagine what had gone on that morning in her life, but that's how visceral the reaction to rejection can be.)

I asked the class: "Would there be any value to life if you never experienced rejection?" Most of the class said yes, so I asked, "How would you go about avoiding rejection for the rest of your life?" I had no idea what the "right" answer was at the time, but the question sure got their attention!

Some of their responses were pretty obvious—never leave home, don't try anything new, stay away from other people, and so on. After a while, silence fell, and one of the boys who sat in the back of the room raised his hand. I was surprised, because the kid hadn't said a word in class all semester. I pointed to him, and the genius of what this seventeen-year-old said still impresses me today.

"Accept yourself first." How powerful is that? Accept yourself first. Don't look to others to accept you. *You* have to accept you. Change begins with and ends with you. This is so powerful it deserves special mention:

> If you want recognition, go outside, and get it from others. If you want true power, go inside yourself, where your God-given resources are abundant.

Garbage In, Garbage Out

Here's the reason why I've spent so much time discussing the brain and how people think: Your perception of yourself—your self-image—comes from your thoughts. Just as you can think and act based on negative input, you can program your brain in a positive way.

How are you thinking now? When's the last time you got up in the morning and said, "Yes! I am awake! I've been blessed with another day! Absolutely anything is possible." Some people get seriously excited about waking up an hour before their alarm goes off. "Oh, thank God! I've got another hour to sleep!" Imagine having a conversation about this in the evening with your significant other:

"What was good about your day, honey?"

"I woke up an hour before the alarm went off and got to go back to sleep! *Yes!*"

Have you ever heard of Dr. Norbert Wiener? He is generally considered to be one of the founding fathers of computer development and is given credit for developing the theory and application of cybernetics, a feedback system in electrons and humans that keeps them on course. More than 60 years ago, he furthered the concept of "garbage in, garbage out" (GIGO)—the output of a computer (behavior) is only as good as its input (attitude).

How does this translate? Stop beating yourself up! When you screw up, saying, "Oh, I am *so* stupid! I always mess it up!" accomplishes *nothing*. Your subconscious doesn't care whether this information is good for you or not. All it can do is record the information and store it for the rest of your life. Tell this to yourself enough times and you'll begin to believe it! It doesn't take long to forget that you're the one who allowed the information in to begin with.

If you don't know better, you tend to focus on what's missing in your life. Most people say that the most important thing in life is good health. But if you asked if they were doing anything to improve their health, few would truthfully say they were exercising on a regular basis or eating healthy foods. Most responses are more along these lines: "Well, I'll get around to it soon. Right now, I'm pretty busy doing other things." When you're sick, what's the one thing that you want? Good health, right? "If I could just be well, I would be eternally happy! I wouldn't ask for another thing!" But where do you draw the line? What is enough? But most of us have our health and yet we say, "I'm still not having the time of my life yet." OOPS.

Garbage in, garbage out. It's true even with the little things. Many people don't consider themselves good at remembering other people's names because they've *convinced themselves* that they aren't good at remembering names. They end up trying to find ways to validate this misconception. Why? Because they want to be right. Here is an example of how we can chase our own tails.

Remembering Names

If you want to be good at remembering people's names, what should you do? Most experts will say you should make an association with the name: "If you meet someone named Al, imagine an alligator over his head." These associations can be inherently problematic: The next time you see Al, you might say, "Hi, Mr. Gator—oh, I mean, Al." Another method is repeating the person's name over and over in your mind or taking a course on remembering.

Once you have convinced yourself that you are *not* good at remembering people's names, you don't have to try to remember to forget them—that will happen naturally. That's what's so amazing about the human thought process—once we let the belief in, it takes over. The person's name is forgotten automatically, so there's no need to consciously try to remember to forget. Is that cool or what?

"Hi, my name's Larry; what's yours?"

"Hi, Larry. My name is—" Suddenly, the sound goes off. Why? Because if you believe that you're not good at remembering people's names, you'll build a scotoma to their names. You'll never even hear it. (This often happens because I'm busy thinking about the next thing I'm going to say, instead of listening to what the other person has to say.) I don't even know I'm doing it. That is the power of a scotoma created by old beliefs.

So how do you get better at remembering names? Simple. Change your belief. Say to yourself, "I am good at remembering names." If I *say* I'm good at remembering names, then I must *act* like I'm good at remembering names. I don't need to

82

figure out how I'm going to remember them, I just need to know that I'm good at remembering them; the "how" will take over naturally. Let's try this again.

"Hi, my name's Larry. What's yours?"

"My name's Tori."

"Tori. How do you spell it?"

"T-O-R-I."

"Is that your full name?"

"No, it's actually Victoria."

"What a beautiful name. Do you know who named you?"

"My mom, I think."

"What's your middle name?"

"Kendal."

"Victoria Kendal, it's a pleasure to meet you."

Why do I ask these questions? To help me remember the name, of course. Once I decide what I want, the "how" appears on its own. I don't have to figure out how first.

The how will always follow the belief, or the belief will be limited to the how.

Remember what you learned about the RAS? The vision comes first, and then you see. You do not see first. Believe first, and put your miraculous God-given brain to work.

Can you see a little more clearly now how much garbage has been programmed into your thinking over the years? The main challenge to your desire to become exceptional—the main thing to be overcome—is your old belief system!

Remember, you can't erase these old beliefs. They're stored in the subconscious for all eternity. *However, you can replace these old beliefs with new, stronger, more positive ones.* Rather than relying on old ways of making decisions based on preconditioned thoughts and attitudes, you can *decide* what you want, and the new attitudes and beliefs will begin to grow. This is the stuff visions are created from, and this is the process we were automatically wired to enjoy. If you don't believe me, watch your children. They can teach you all about what we've let ourselves give up.

The G.A.P.™ of Opportunity

You make decisions based on your self-image. So what decisions should you make? *Ones that support your new vision of yourself.*

So how can you start doing that immediately? Consider the example of me asking you to sing. If you review the decision-making process, you'll find that once you were asked to "sing," you perceived, associated, evaluated, and then decided. But you usually don't make decisions based on opportunity or vision; instead, you make decisions based on past conditioning. In this particular case, this past conditioning is based on how others have experienced you as a singer, and how you've experienced yourself as a singer. The opportunity to change occurs instantly when you realize that you have a choice. You don't have to act as you always have before. Instead, you can choose a new, more desirable behavior.

"So what," you might say. "Who cares? What difference does that make?" It makes a huge difference. Because you have a cerebral cortex, you aren't stuck with the simple fight-or-flight mechanism kicking in from your amygdala. Instead, you can *choose* your behavior, whenever you want.

When you recognize and become aware that this is possible, you create what I call the *G.A.P. of Opportunity.* G.A.P. stands for Gaining Additional Performance. You end up getting more out of life than you expected.

When I'm in a situation I don't like, or I'm feeling like my ability to perform well is limited, I can break my conditioning instantly by asking the following question: *"How do I want to be right now?"* Instantaneously, I'm transformed from what I have become into what I want to become. I'm now in the creative zone and working with fresh and extremely pliable neurons. Remember, when you ask yourself that question, there is only one unacceptable answer: "I don't know. Anyone would feel the same way."

You're not "anyone," and you're in no danger of firing new neurons if you keep responding to what you've always done. The whole point of free will is to improve your life. Living in the G.A.P. creates new choices and puts you in a position to enjoy your life to the fullest, *right now.*

Remember, process always follows vision! Don't try to first create a process and then come up with a vision. Never say, "We've got a great plan, so let's find out what we can do with it." Create your vision first. I don't need to learn how to be good at remembering people's names, do I? No, I just need to decide that I am already good at remembering people's names! If you learned the name of every living person in the world, the area of brain cells required would be about as large as a pea. Since the brain is capable of remembering billions of names, don't you think it can handle the few hundred names of the people you regularly come in contact with?

A Final Note

You can't simply want to change; you must know *how* to change. The "how" begins with your thought process—what you program your brain to believe. Success isn't about "if" you can do something. It occurs because you *know* you can. High-performance people *know that they can know*. They don't need to know how; they simply decide what they want to do or become, and the "how" comes naturally.

The beginning step is always to ask yourself, *"What do I want?"* If you don't already know, ask yourself what you *don't* want. Once you've decided what you don't want, you're ready to ask yourself what you do want.

It all goes back to having a clear vision.

Lesson 3
Reflection Questions

What beliefs do you have about yourself that are holding you back personally or professionally?

How can applying the G.A.P. of Opportunity improve your decision making?

Think of a current challenge in your life. How has looking in the rear-view mirror kept you from overcoming this challenge?

How could you overcome this challenge by imagining what life would look like without it? Where would the "how" come from?

Why is it detrimental to try to change another human being?

How can you accelerate your performance by becoming aware of the OOPS formula?

I take away the following insight from this lesson …

I intend to use it first in the areas of ...

Because ...

List the behaviors you would like to change or visions you would like to accomplish:

Lesson 4: The Most Powerful Force on the Planet: Attitude

"We don't see things as they are;
we see things as we are." —Anaïs Nin

This lesson focuses on how we have come to think of ourselves and others the way that we do. We'll examine the power of the "inner voice" (which I call Rox-Talk™) that we pay so much attention to. We'll also discover that what we think of ourselves is not influenced by what we see, hear, or read—instead, it is most influenced by how we *talk to ourselves* about what we see, hear, or read. In other words, what we allow ourselves to do is seldom based on what is possible for us. More often than not, it is based on what we have come to expect of ourselves.

Before we jump into Lesson 4, I want to bring up another important point. You've already learned that your self-image is stored in your subconscious. Pay close attention to the impact of this next idea, because it is essential for vision accomplishment and high self-esteem: *your subconscious does not know the difference between an actual experience and one that you simply think about.* In other words, whenever you think about something and feel an emotion, your subconscious records the experience as if it were actually happening to you now.

We haven't always relied on our thinking to influence our attitudes and behavior, have we? No—in infancy, humans think purely with emotion. A baby is a totally emotive creature. It derives no sense of self from its environment. If a baby is warm and dry and her belly is full, she's happy. Everything is amazing. She wears an expression of pure wonderment.

This emotive state doesn't last. We begin to learn. Babies begin to identify pictures after only a few months. A few short months later, they are able to finish the process by learning words.

Adults think in the opposite direction. If personal growth is important to you, always remember this: *We think with words, and words trigger pictures in our brains. These pictures generate emotions, and emotions cause us to take action.* Of course, the "action" that is chosen may be to do nothing. But 99 times out of 100, attitude causes us to continue doing what we are used to doing, without ever having to try something new—even if what we are doing is not good for us.

Therefore, language has a powerful effect on behavior. In the science of psycholinguistics, the power that language has on our behavior is called *self-talk*. I've come up with a new term for self-talk: Rox-Talk.™ (You'll understand why soon.) As discussed earlier, it is frustrating, counterproductive, and more often than not, only effective in the short term to try to change behavior, because subconscious attitudes drive behavior.

If that's the case, how do we change our attitudes? If you don't know how to change your attitude, it's probably because you don't know how you acquired it in the first place. But if you do know how you acquired your attitudes, you can use the same process to change the attitudes that don't get you what you want into attitudes that do. This is what Lesson 4 is all about.

Who's Driving Your Car?

An attitude is a predetermined response to a given stimulus. But let's consider a definition that makes more sense as we move from the term self-talk to the new one, Rox-Talk. Your attitude is the direction in which you lean. Attitudes aren't necessarily good or bad, or right or wrong—they're simply the direction you lean toward.

Let's get a little more into this definition of an attitude. The term *predetermined* refers to all the similar experiences stored in your subconscious. *Stimuli* are the "things" that trigger one or more of your senses. When you're affected by a stimulus, you respond based on something similar in your past—an experience, perhaps, or thoughts you may have had. You're definitely not born with attitudes. You learn them.

Imagine that you are carrying two buckets of water, and the buckets are balanced by a wooden pole or yoke resting across your shoulders and back. As long as the buckets contain equal amounts of water, they are level. But if one bucket has more water in it, what happens? Everything leans in that direction.

The same thing is true about attitudes. In your mind, label one of those buckets "positive attitude" and the other "negative attitude." Now, if the positive bucket has more water, you've got a positive attitude, and if negative bucket has more water, you've got a negative attitude. If I tell all my friends that I love the opera, buy season tickets to it, and attend every performance, I have a positive attitude about opera. If I lean the other way— I tell everyone that I can't stand opera, that it all seems like a lot of yelling in a foreign language, and that it makes no sense to me, I have a negative attitude about opera. Again, notice something important here: Whether I like or don't like opera doesn't make me "right" or "wrong"—it's simply the direction in which I lean.

So who's driving your car (that is, your life)? If you think it's your behavior, followed by your attitudes, you're wrong. Your attitudes drive your behavior.

The Roxometer™

Aperneo has developed an acronym that mimics what happens neurologically in your brain whenever someone says something to you, or when you say something to yourself. Whenever anything happens to us, we register one experience, which we call ROX.

R   Registering
O   One
X   Xperience

We measure the total sum of these experiences with the Roxometer.™ Picture yourself carrying those buckets of water again. Positive thoughts and experiences go in the positive bucket, negative thoughts and experiences go in the other.

Rox-Talk™

Your Rox-Talk is vitally important to your success in life for two reasons:

1. We're thinking almost all the time. We think twenty-four hours a day, seven days a week. Don't believe me? Try to get away from thinking sometime. Even if you have been thinking quite a bit and feel exhausted, you can still go on thinking, can't you? What happens at night when you try to stop thinking so you can get some sleep? "If I keep this conversation up, I'll be exhausted in the morning!" When you say something like that to yourself, your brain just laughs at you.

   "Look how he is using me! I've got all these untapped neurons just sitting around with nothing to do, and he thinks that if he doesn't stop thinking, he'll wake up tired!" You can only end up where your thinking takes you. There are really only two things that will make you truly tired: Working or exercising so long and hard that you're physically exhausted, or spending too much time thinking about how difficult life is, and mentally wearing yourself out.

2. We've touched on this before, but I want to emphasize it again: your subconscious mind cannot distinguish between comments that others make and comments you think or make to yourself. Your subconscious doesn't just react to actual experiences, it also reacts to your thoughts—*and it can't distinguish between the two!*

Now, does one stray thought lead to a belief? Probably not, unless you have a great deal of emotion associated with that thought. Thoughts accumulate over time to create beliefs.

Let me tell you another story that demonstrates how thoughts create attitudes or beliefs. In 1957, I was nine years old and lived in the Seattle suburb of Tacoma, Washington. One day, my parents called me into the living room of our house. My dad told me, "Larry, we'd like to give you the opportunity to see what music is all about for you. What instrument would you like to play?"

Many parents encourage their children to get involved in as many things as possible—including such pursuits as athletics and music. If the child becomes engaged in the activity, they usually encourage it even more. Note that my father never asked me, "Do you want to play an instrument?" because I probably would've said "No." He wasn't interested in a "no," so he asked, "What do you want to play?"

I replied, "An accordion."

My response was greeted with some serious negative attitudes. My father said, "The accordion? How on earth are you going to be in the marching band playing the accordion?" Clearly, his vision was for me to be in the marching band. My mother added, "Can't you at least try the piano instead? Why the accordion, of all things?"

I didn't know then that we are all products of our conditioning. At the time, there was a popular Saturday-morning kids' show called the *Stan Borison Show*. Stan played the accordion. I wanted to play the accordion because I associated playing the accordion with having fun.

My parents honored my request, and Grandma bought me a forty-pound black Petosa accordion, a top-of-the-line model. They also set me up with a series of weekly lessons from a gentleman named Herb Erickson. Erickson was cool—not only did he play accordion in a big band, but he also had his own music stands with "H.E." on them. As far as I was concerned, he was the Michael Jordan of accordion players.

The first week, Erickson assigned me a piece of music, and I had a week to practice it. When it came time for the next lesson, I lugged my 40-pound accordion the six blocks to Erickson's house. As soon as we settled into his den, Erickson asked, "Larry, why don't you play the song for me?"

During the previous week, I'd developed a negative attitude about practicing the accordion. I was outside playing when I should've been practicing. So when Erickson asked me to play the song, I said, "Why don't you go ahead and play it first?" I was stalling—I knew what would happen when he discovered that I hadn't practiced.

Erickson played the song, and by the time he'd finished, I'd discovered my gift. Everyone has a gift of some kind, but our society teaches that if you don't have to work hard for something, it has no value. Hence a lot of people don't value their gifts. My gift, I found, is that I can hear a song and play it. I can't teach anybody else this skill, but I sure have it. Now, I didn't play the song well enough to stop writing this book and play professionally, but I played it well enough to impress Erickson, particularly considering I was a beginner.

When I finished my rendition of the song, Erickson exclaimed, "Larry! That was really good! You're a good little musician!"

What happened next? Well, let's think about this for a minute. Remember the water buckets: One bucket was marked positive, the other was negative. We're born with billions of empty, neutral buckets. Thoughts equal ROX, so what we think about or what happens to us and we think about it are our ROX. When Erickson said, "Larry, you're a good little musician," ROX were dropped into my positive bucket. That's not all—the entire way home I told myself, "I *am* a great little musician, man! Herb really liked my playing! That was pretty cool!" More ROX in my positive bucket, right? The process was beginning. I was developing a belief and an attitude that I was a good musician, and no one could tell me otherwise.

Fast-forward a year and a half to what was to become my last lesson with Erickson. By that point, I was really a hot little accordion player. I had played in contests, I had played at universities, and my accordion was covered in award decals. When it came to playing the accordion, I was cooking with gas.

Here's how powerful Rox-Talk can be. I was still doing the old routine of not practicing and simply listening to Erickson and repeating what he played. He must've suspected something, however, because this time, he played the song with several mistakes. Since I'd never heard the song before, I played it exactly as he had, mistakes and all.

Erickson became incensed. "Ha! I thought so!" he yelled. "You can't read music. What's more, you will *never* be a great musician!"

Now here's an extremely critical point: *ROX don't drop into our buckets unless we agree with them.* Remember that. You must sanction the ROX. When Herb flew into a rage at me, I could have said, in my own mind, "What do you know, Herb? I'll show you!" Many of us have done just that to coaches, teachers, parents, and others along the way, haven't we? But I didn't, because Herb had caught me, in my own mind, red-handed. I agreed with him. What do you think determines the size of the ROX in each bucket?

> The size of each ROX equals the emotion attached to it.

If I'm neutral, and somebody puts a marble in one of my buckets and a sixteen-pound boulder in the other bucket, which is going to have the most impact? The boulder. Boom! My Roxometer tips right over. Erickson dumped a boulder in my negative bucket that day. On the six mile walk home, carrying what felt like a 400 pound accordion with tears in my eyes, I thought to myself, "You're terrible. You never learned how to read music. You played when you should have been practicing. What did you expect?" I'd gone from the top of the world to having a completely negative attitude about being a musician.

You're probably thinking. "That was over 40 years ago. Get over it!" But it's not that easy. At least that's what I thought then.

Let me tell you how that attitude about myself as a musician followed me along in life. In 1966, I was in a rock band called The Regents. (Rock bands always had cool names, but unfortunately the Beatles and Stones had already used up the great names.) Anyway, we were the only rock band where the piano player—that would be me—was way off in the background, tucked away behind the drums. I was hiding! My electric piano's volume was regulated by an amplifier. My band mates would turn me up, I'd turn me down, they'd turn me up again, and I'd turn me down again. I was convinced that I wasn't a very good musician. In my opinion, a good musician studied the classics, learned the "right way," and had a right to be playing like he did. Compared to someone like that, I was nothing.

Watch out for comparisons. We feel good when we feel we're better than others, but we feel lousy when we think that we're worse than them. Remember, who else in this world is just like you? Nobody. Be careful when you try to be like others, or even compare yourself to them: you can't be anyone other than who you are, and by the time you've finished this book, you won't want to be, anyway.

To the Cliff House

Let me continue this idea by telling you another story about the power of Rox-Talk. Fast-forward to 1971. I had just graduated from college, was looking for a job, and heard about an opening teaching at a junior high school in Bremerton, Washington. I got the job and signed a contract to make $8,200 for the school year— about $550 take-home pay each month. With all that money, I had to buy a new car, so I purchased a 12-year-old Volkswagen on its fourth engine.

At one point in its long life, it had been royal blue, but by then the paint had faded to a powder blue. I also put some money down on 24-foot mobile home, because I needed a place to live, of course. School started, and I was happy, going back and forth to work, grading papers at night, and making money doing something I loved. Life was good.

One day, I got a call from an old and very dear friend of mine named Jim. He was working as a bartender at a restaurant called the Cliff House, a beautiful restaurant situated 500 feet above Puget Sound. It was a very swanky place with a revolving piano bar.

Jim told me, "Larry, the piano player here is sick. Why don't you come over and audition?"

"Are you out of your mind?" I said.

"What are you talking about? You and I jam all the time!" (Jim thought he was a harmonica player, and I thought I was a piano player, so we would get together and jam. But that's as far as it went.)

Jim said, "Come on! It can't hurt to try."

"Sorry, Jim. I've got too many things to do. I've got all these papers to grade." (We get really creative when we don't want to do something, right?)

Next, he caught my attention: "Larry, it pays $300 a weekend!"

"Tell me more," I said.

He asked, "What's the worst thing that can happen?"

"Well, the worst thing that could happen would be if they hired me. That's the worst thing that could happen."

But Jim persisted. "Come on," he said. "Stop by and I'll buy you a soda." Eventually, I relented. I drove down to the Cliff House. I greeted Jim and caught up with him for a while until the owner came over. We chatted for a few moments, and then the owner said, "Well, play me a song."

"What do you want to hear?"

"Georgia on My Mind."

Luckily, I knew that particular song. When I was finished, the owner said something that absolutely terrified me. "You're hired. Be here tonight at nine sharp."

I immediately began experiencing cognitive dissonance, the disharmony that occurs when you try to hold two conflicting thoughts in your mind at the same time. In this case, I wanted the money, but I didn't want to have to play the piano in front of anyone to get it. Can you imagine the stress I was under?

So the next thing I knew, it was nine that evening and I was sitting behind the keys in the middle of a revolving piano bar. I was all dressed up and scared to death.

A patron sat down and said, "What's wrong?" What's wrong? Was he out of his mind? I would rather have been someplace—practically anyplace—else! *That's* what's wrong! I couldn't tell him that, of course, but that's how I felt. I honestly didn't know how I was going to make it through the evening.

I learned about a crutch that night, something that helps you out when you are way out of your comfort zone and all stressed out: alcohol. A patron bought me a drink, I accepted, and the next thing I knew, there was an orange drink sitting next to me on the piano. I took a sip and it tasted just like orange juice, except different. (I later found out it was a Screwdriver.)

The night began pretty well, and other patrons bought me Screwdrivers. I wasn't much of a drinker, so by the end of the night, I was playing every song requested and singing, too! (We don't need to get into what kind of attitude I had about myself as a singer.) When the bar closed, the owner came up to me. "Larry," he said, "we had an incredible night! You were terrific. Here's your tip-jar money."

Tip jar? I didn't know I had a tip jar. It materialized out of nowhere. We counted out the money, and guess what? There was $150 in the tip jar, on top of the $150 I made for playing that night. I'd just made $300 in one night. I was only taking home $550 a month teaching school, so as far as I was concerned, I was rich.

Then the owner said, "Our regular piano player is still sick. Can you come back tomorrow night?" When I woke up the next morning with a bit of a hangover, I remembered agreeing to do just that.

Now I was really in trouble. Remember, I believed that my musical abilities were terrible. Herb Erickson, the Michael Jordan of the accordion world, told me I'd never be a good musician, and he should know! Those people at the bar were just being nice. *Remember, when we lock on, we only accept information that matches our beliefs.* Everything else is locked out. There was no way that my attitude would let me believe that I was a musician. OOPS!

I'm not proud of what I did before my next shift at the Cliff House. I went to a liquor store. At the time, I was quite a price shopper, so I picked out the cheapest bottle of vodka I could find (kerosene probably has a smoother flavor!), went back to my mobile home, and made a little pitcher of Screwdrivers. I had a couple of drinks in the parking lot before I entered the Cliff House, and the next thing I knew I had made it through another night. The same thing happened—I had made another $150 just in tips! It was another $300 night—$600 in two nights! (Looking back, I'm sure the owner had something to do with the amount in the tip jar, because two nights with the exact same tip money...well, don't you think that's a little suspicious?)

After that second night, the owner said, "Larry, guess what? I fired the piano player! We're sold out next weekend! Congratulations, you are our new piano player."

I was freaked out. I was *petrified*. And the owner said, "Hey, I know this is sudden."

And I said, "I can't be your piano..."

"Don't go there yet!" he said. "Just think about it. Have a nice Sunday tomorrow and I'll call you next week."

I was in pretty deep now, but I quickly got in deeper. On Monday the owner called me up and said, "Larry, I know you're just thinking about being the piano player here, but do you mind if someone comes over to your school and takes your picture while you're thinking about it?" (You've seen those signs at the entrance to the lounge that say: "Now Appearing So-and-So.")

I said, "There's no way... "

"I'll send the photographer over to the school. It won't take but a moment of your time. Will Wednesday be fine?"

On Wednesday, the principal paged me. "Mr. Olsen, please come to the office." A photographer from the local newspaper was waiting for me. I thought to myself, "What is the *Tribune* doing here?" I was trying to make sense of all this, but I didn't ask too many questions. I figured the photographer was a friend of the owner's, doing him a favor. So we went to the school auditorium, I sat next to the piano, and the photographer snapped away.

The rest of Wednesday went by and I didn't hear from the owner. Thursday went by, no call from the owner. I certainly wasn't going to call *him*, because I was avoiding conflict, just like my mother taught me. When she'd get upset with me, she wouldn't talk to me. This was very effective because I loved her very much, but it is the ostrich approach to conflict resolution—sticking your head in the sand and hoping the problem goes away.

That Friday morning, I was eating my breakfast and leafing through the paper before I went to work. Something caught my eye in the paper's weekend section. It was an ad for the Cliff House—with a picture of me. The headline screamed, "Playing and Singing at the Cliff House: Larry Olsen!"

Singing? Uh oh. I had a big problem on my hands. I had gone to grade school in Tacoma. I had gone to high school in Tacoma. Now, everyone in Tacoma would be at the Cliff House that weekend, to make fun of the new piano player. Not good attitudes to have, are they?

I hate to admit this, too, but I will: I didn't go back to the Cliff House. That morning, the owner called and I told him I was sick. He thought I was trying to negotiate for more money, but eventually he realized that I wasn't going to come in that day, or any other day, for that matter. "Larry, if you don't come in tonight," he said, "I never want to see you in my restaurant again."

He never saw me in the restaurant again. Attitudes last until you change them. *If you don't learn to change your attitude, you'll change your opportunity every single time, whether it's good for you or not.* Of course, sometimes you learn other routes to compensate and get by. I could've compensated, easily, by keeping the screwdrivers coming. Alcohol is in no danger of changing your attitude, but it can definitely change your life. I'd rather have a drink because I *choose to* rather than have a drink because I *need to* in order to get through something.

Don't Think About ...

Every attitude you have has a Roxometer above it, leaning you in a certain direction. I want to emphasize this point again: Thoughts accumulate to build beliefs. You have a thought every 1.7 seconds. That's more than fifty thousand ROX per day. You cannot change or break an old habit or attitude by telling yourself *not* to do something, because the subconscious doesn't follow directions. It follows words

Let me give you an example. Whatever you do, do not follow my words, follow my directions: Don't, I repeat, *don't* think about a black dog with white ears in a red doghouse. How did you do? Did you follow my directions or did you follow my words? Why didn't you think instead about a yellow snake slithering through green grass? Because people don't follow directions, we follow words. Remember this:

> When talking to yourself or another, only talk about what you want, not about what you don't.

Why is this so true? Because either way you are dropping ROX. What bucket do you want to drop them in? *Thoughts are ROX. ROX drop into buckets. Buckets become your attitude. Attitude is measured by your Roxometer. What direction do you want your Roxometer to take you?* **Then think in that direction.**

Thoughts are getting dropped into your Roxometer buckets right at this very moment. Ask yourself, "How am I thinking about what I am doing? Where am I dropping these ROX? Am I reinforcing an attitude I don't like without knowing it, or am I creating a new one?"

Change Attitude or Opportunity?

Anyone can break through to success simply by changing their thoughts, attitudes, and behaviors, in that order. Business leaders don't need to change their people. Instead, they need to change their attitudes about *their* people. If you change your attitudes about others, they'll change right before your eyes. Why? Because they are being treated differently now.

Successful business leaders only want one thing from their people—a fresh perspective—and the only way they will get it is if they create fresh perspectives about their people. You get into a grind after a while by doing the same old thing with the same old people. It's always so refreshing when a new person joins the team without a lot of baggage. Soon enough, even those new people get pegged one way or another.

Mahatma Gandhi said, "You must be the change you wish to see in the world." If I bring out the best in you, you will treat me as I treat you. Leaders must be able to change their opinions about their employees, when they do, their employees' performance will rise.

If you're not currently a leader, what can you do? You can change your attitudes about *your* leaders, for one thing. And if you are truly looking for positive growth, the most important attitude to change is the one you have about yourself. What's your attitude about yourself? Is it refreshing? Do you love what you're doing and who you're with? If not, learn how to change your attitude or you'll change your job and the people you're with, and unfortunately end up bringing the same you to the next opportunity.

A Final Note

In *Hamlet*, Shakespeare wrote, "There is nothing either good or bad, but thinking makes it so." Thinking controls our behavior in every facet of our lives. Our thoughts can be negative or positive, and whether they are negative or positive depends on our attitudes.

If you're ever resisting anything, recognize that you've got an attitude that may need changing. There's not necessarily anything wrong, but your attitude won't allow you to see information that doesn't support it. *What we dislike most in others is what we dislike most in ourselves. What I like most about you is what I like most about myself.* This fundamental principle can teach us, through others, which attitudes we need to change in ourselves.

You can change your attitude the same way that you created it—by changing how you think about experiences. When you begin to change how you think, an important change will take place within you. You will shed the shell you've worn all these years—the shell your parents, your siblings, your community, and others created around you. *You will begin to peel away your preconditioning and your learned behaviors and let the real, miraculous, one-of-a-kind you out.*

Change your attitudes and you'll change your life. It's really quite simple. What's difficult about change is not the change itself; it's only a misperception of difficulty that makes it difficult. How do you want it to be? Simple or difficult? Once you decide, the results will follow. Be careful what you think about, though, or...OOPS!

Lesson 4
Reflection Questions

What are the things you've done that you're most proud of?

_____

_____

_____

What do you want to say to yourself about the following areas of your life?

Intelligence:

_____

Body:

_____

Spouse/Significant Other:

_____

Work:

_____

Balance in Life:

_____

Happiness:

_____

How Others See Me:

_____

Financial Situation:

_____

Spirituality:

_____

What are you going to do that you're not already doing now to assure that the above "wants" become reality?

_____

_____

_____

How were your attitudes formed, and how can you positively affect your Roxometer?

_____

_____

_____

Among the people you know, who needs their self-esteem raised the most, and how can you help?

_____

_____

_____

_____

I take away the following insight from this lesson …

I intend to use it first in the areas of …

Because …

List the behaviors you would like to change or visions you would like to accomplish:

Lesson 5: The Five Easy S.T.E.P.S. to Prosperity

"Let us not go over the old grounds; let us rather prepare for what is to come." —Cicero (106–43 B.C.)

What happens when we create new attitudes? Old attitudes never disappear, but the new ones, in effect, overwrite the old. The old attitudes become faded and don't have the same value they had before.

Next, we'll focus specifically on how you can begin to create new attitudes by filling the positive bucket of your Roxometer with boulders and poking holes in your negative bucket. Why would anyone who knows better put ROX in the negative bucket, anyway?

How Do We Change?

The key to change is to have a *vision* of the end result you desire. There is no single vision—all of us have several visions. The power of each vision must be so strong that you can't keep doing what you've been doing and expect to accomplish it … unless what you're doing is on track to your vision.

Each of us have a few visions, but we have many goals. Visions are the completed pictures of what we want, and goals are the steps we take to get there. For instance, one of my visions is to be a lean, keen, change-agent machine. My goals to reach that vision include attaining my desired weight, eating the right foods, exercising regularly, and so on. My one vision includes many goals.

People want change because they become dissatisfied in some area of their lives. Thus, the easiest route to change is to change your self-image.

Trying to change via willpower is a nicer way of saying that we are using our power to will ourselves to become something other than what we've become. It's the most common—and the hardest—method of change. Why? Because it involves behaving differently than we currently do, and our bodies are wired to stay the same. If the self-image doesn't change, all of our habits, attitudes, beliefs, and expectations, which are stored in our subconscious, are all programmed to keep us the same. This is why 95 percent of diets fail, and why personal change has gotten such a bad rap. Who wants to go to all the trouble of changing, when it's so much easier to stay the same?

An Absolutely Incredible Idea

Why don't you work *with* the system rather than *against* it? Work with me here. Since self-image automatically keeps you the same, and your self-image makes you do what you do without even having to think about it (remember, the only time you have to think about your behavior is when you are trying to change it), then why don't you change your self-image? You can stay the same, but that "same" now becomes what you want it to be, rather than what it has become. *You can become what you've always wanted to be without having to work harder or smarter. Instead, you'll just learn how to think differently.*

S.T.E.P.S.

My formula for successful change is so easy that you already know how to use it. This formula will show you the proper S.T.E.P.S. to vision accomplishment and high self-esteem. To create new self-images that replace your old ones, automatically achieving new results in all the areas you choose, just take these easy S.T.E.P.S.:

S. Strategic Thinking

Strategic thinking takes place whenever you are thinking about what you want. When you think about what you want, what's usually the first question that pops into your mind? "How can I make this vision a reality?" But wondering how you can accomplish your vision is the worst thing you can do, because you're limiting yourself. Right now you don't know *how*...but you will later. If you think you already know how, you've probably developed an attitude about the how, or you'd already be there.

Focusing on the "how" can also create obstacles. You can get bogged down quickly with all the things standing in your way. You might think, "*I* have to change? What happened the last time I tried to change?" In this first step, focus only on what you want in a specific area, and don't worry about how you're going to get it.

T. Think on It

Think on what? *What you want.* Perhaps you, like me, want to become a lean, keen, change-agent machine. If so, you've got to *think on it.* Be specific. What do I look like? How am I going to be different? What am I going to be wearing? How am I going to perceive myself? What's the most exciting change that will occur as a result of accomplishing my vision? *As I think on it, so it is.* As the Book of Proverbs 23:7 states, "As a man thinketh in his heart, so is he."

Philippians 4:8 has another powerful passage, which nails what I mean by *thinking on it*: "Finally, brethren, whatever things are true, whatever things are noble, whatever things are just, whatever things are pure, whatever things are lovely, whatever things are of good report, if there is any virtue and if there is anything praiseworthy—meditate on these things... ." Don't dwell on what's wrong, either about yourself or another. Instead, dwell on what's right! Break the negative conditioning and start valuing yourself.

In addition to its better known meaning, "sin" is also an archer's term for missing the mark. That old statement of "go and sin no more"—what's it really saying? Get over it! Move on! Maybe you messed up, but haven't we all? The next step—and you need to get to it quickly—is to focus on what you want to feel like once it becomes a reality.

E. Emotionalize It

The size of the ROX in your Roxometer is determined by the amount of emotion you've attached to it. Thus, you must emotionalize your vision. Buy it a flower, take it out to dinner, and romance it. Give yourself the opportunity to be playful. Imagine it. Have some fun.

When you do, your conscious mind will probably rebel. "What the heck are you doing? Are you crazy?" Why does this back-talk occur in response to your Rox-Talk? The back-talk is trying to keep you the same and maintain your old sanity—"Don't you forget who you are." You are wired to maintain your sanity at any cost. You will soon learn to enjoy your internal back-talk rather than continue to get kicked down by it. *Imagine talking yourself into something rather than out of something.*

As you attempt to change, you are moving against what you've become, but you can change that easily by staying in the vision. When I emotionalize my vision, guess what I'm doing? Every time I think about my vision with the positive emotion attached, I drop a ROX in my positive bucket. That's great, but guess what else I'm doing? I'm firing new neurons. I'm creating new neurological patterns that will cause my behavior to match or otherwise sync with the new vision. You don't need a prefrontal lobotomy to try to forget about the things that you don't want to remember anymore. It's all about vision, and the positive emotions you can attach to it. When you focus on the new, you become dissatisfied with the old.

This is simple, but extremely powerful, information. As Henry Ford said, "Whether I think I can, or think I can't, I'm right." Create the vision, and then begin to emotionalize it by feeling like you've already achieved it. As we look forward to something we want, we create positive emotions. Our RAS always gathers the information necessary to make certain that we stay the same, and our behavior follows our vision. By changing our vision, we automatically change our behavior. Now the "same" you is a higher-level you.

This is where habits come into play. We tend to think the same way over and over, whether it's good for us or not. We try to stop or change the habits that don't lead us to our visions, but simply stopping a habit is the worst approach you can take. Why? Because the more you resist anything, the greater it persists. You have told yourself what's important to you, so your RAS is wide open only to what you think is significant.

The same principle applies when we give directions to another person. You and I don't follow directions, we follow words. (They trigger pictures, which bring about emotion.) In the last lesson, when I asked you to *not* think about a black dog with white ears in a red doghouse, what did you do? Of course—you thought about a white-eared black dog in a red doghouse. Did you follow my directions—what I asked you *not* to do—or did you follow my words?

What does all this mean? Simply this: Tell people what you *want*, not what you *don't want*.

This: "Susan, please show us how fast you are."

Not this: "Susan, don't slow us down."

We struggle with this concept all the time, don't we? Gary Latham, a professor of organizational effectiveness at Toronto University, studied the effects of performance evaluations on employees. He interviewed people at hundreds of U.S. corporations and learned that it took employees, on average, *three months* to get back to the level of performance they'd achieved before the review took place. Their reviews demoralized them, and even people who received primarily positive reviews usually focused on the review's criticisms. It's no different than a third-grader getting homework back with mistakes circled in red. A kid can answer 99 questions correctly and focus on the single one he or she got wrong. Same goes for a performance review, if you don't know any better.

When you emotionalize the vision, it must come from the value you perceive, rather than the emotion generated by imagining the work involved. When it comes to performance, there's a huge difference between the two.

P. Picture

Once you've created, thought about, and emotionalized your vision, you create a new neurological pattern or picture, and this new picture will in turn change your behavior.

Rather than just hanging the new picture on your mirror or on the side of your refrigerator, hang it on the wall of your subconscious. Create a new neurological state—a new self-image—through the repetition of imagining the new reality or vision. What drives behavior? Self-image. What determines your sanity? Self-image.

Remember:

> High-performance people live their vision as if they have already achieved it.

That brings us to the last letter of S.T.E.P.S. and the beginning of new behaviors.

S. Self-Image

The objective (as well as assuring the results we want) takes place when you have created a new self-image. Each time you think about what you want, dwell on it, and feel the emotion, you record the experience as if it's actually happening to you. This creates a new picture of what you want, thus creating a new self-image. Behavior changes automatically, because self-image drives behavior. So as you think and emotionalize, you drop ROX increasing the "lean" in your attitude because increasing the emotion increases the speed of the change, which in turn creates the new attitude. *You move towards and become that which you think about. Your present thoughts determine your future.*

S.T.E.P.S. creates success because you're creating new self-images. As you do, your RAS will find the information necessary for your ultimate vision accomplishment.

Having Fun While You're Growing

Growing is fun, or it should be, anyway, because nothing's more fun than imagining what you want. Nothing is more fulfilling than achieving it. The flip-side, however, is not dreaming big enough, because nothing brings you down more than falling short of your vision.

We tend to give up too easily, don't we? Three times and we're out. "I tried. I did, I really tried that time. No, I'm serious, I really did try. I even went out and bought all the equipment. I did. I went through the L.I.F.E. Program, and I even read the book!"

Imagine that your vision is to get into good physical shape by running. You run out and buy all the equipment: shoes, cool shorts, and water-repellant running gear. You decide that a lack of time or bad weather won't be acceptable excuses anymore. You've been getting up at seven a.m. for ten years, but now, you're going to start getting up at six to run. You are motivated!

Samuel Johnson wrote, "The road to Hell is paved with good intentions." In this case, change becomes a living Hell. Hell isn't a destination, it's how you live your life. The moral of this story is, live your *vision* and change will be natural, or live the *process* and change can be Hell.

In the above example about getting in shape, you have no vision. You have a plan, a process, and a lot of equipment, but no vision. When you have a vision, you don't have to talk yourself into doing anything. You can't wait to get started.

However, in the example, you do have a goal—to run. This next point is crucial to your understanding of vision: the vision is the ultimate reason *why* you're running. Goals aren't enough. *To attain the most fulfilling successes in life, goals must be part of a bigger picture and a bigger result*. They must be a road to your vision, the steps necessary to arrive at the new you.

Stop Affirming What You *Don't* Want

Having a strong, clear vision allows you to relax and have fun along the way, because if you know where you're going, you'll be confident that the S.T.E.P.S. you're taking will assure your arrival. Therefore, you can enjoy yourself! I hope you're beginning to see that this isn't difficult, and in fact, it's actually quite easy. Once you change by creating a vision, your attitude changes, and you develop new, positive habits. Your RAS opens itself up to all of the information necessary to accomplish your new "reality," and as a result, your behavior changes automatically.

With this in mind, here's another important point to remember:

> Having a vision is so powerful, relative to the life you are currently living, that you must make sure that you only have visions for things that you want to have or become, not what you want to move away from.

Most of us attempt to change by backing away from something we don't like, rather than growing toward something we do. Unfortunately, whenever we back away from what we don't want, we create "worry." This is how many people operate constantly. *We can create new attitudes*. Remember to create new ones that are worthy of who you are instead of creating new attitudes that are based on what you've become.

The 10

The next exercise will show you the power of a clear, compelling vision that you can apply S.T.E.P.S. toward. Don't cop a negative attitude about this: It isn't "homework," and you don't "have to" do it. But if you do this exercise, you'll discover the power of vision first-hand and take your first step toward having the time of your life, *right now.*

I want you to think about the following question. You don't have to share your thoughts with anyone else.

What would have to happen for tonight to be one of the top 10 most wonderful nights of your life?

Think about it. On a scale of one to 10, with a one being the absolute worst night of your life and a 10 being one of the most fulfilling nights of your life, what would have to happen?

Today's date and time (If you're reading this just before you fall asleep, put tomorrow's date and pick a time.):

What would have to happen?

Has anybody in the history of the world experienced that particular date before? No. Have you ever lived through this time before? No. But you probably think you already know what tonight will be like, don't you? You figure it will go pretty much the same as every other night. When you put your head on the pillow tonight, you'll think, "Yep, this evening went just about as I expected."

What's even sadder is that many people, after reading the question, would think, "If I'm going to dream up one of the top 10 nights of my life, could we pick another night?" Since no one in the history of the earth has ever experienced tonight yet, how could anyone say that?

Here's another question. If you could have any number you wanted for this evening —with one being a loser night and 10 an absolutely incredible night—without having to plan anything new or different, pretty much anyone would pick the perfect 10 evening.

Here's the exercise that I want you to do tonight: I am going to give you a 10 for this evening. It's yours. You didn't have to do anything to get it. *Your job tonight is simply to not let life take it away, and don't let anyone else know what you're doing.* Don't tell your spouse or significant other, your friends, or your children. You can't tell anybody you're doing this. I simply want you to have a 10 evening in your mind, and I also want you to observe whether life's happening to you, or you're happening to life.

If you lived through this evening without a number—with no vision, guess what would happen? Let's say you get in your car to go home and find that your tire's flat. "There goes my 10...now I've got a nine!" You look in the trunk and you realize that the flat tire you have is already your spare tire. "I'm down to a seven and dropping fast!"

You finally get another tire and you're on your way home. It's late, and during the entire drive all you hear on the radio is bad news. By the time you get home, you bring a one of an evening home to your family. No matter how high the ratings of your family members' evenings, the moment before you walked in the door, you were about to erode their numbers. That's how powerful you are.

Keeping the 10

So tonight, no matter what happens to you, simply say the following: Instead of "there goes my 10!" think, *"How can I make this a part of my 10?"* each and every time something happens. Remember, "I don't know; anyone would be upset in this situation," is always an unacceptable answer. You're not just "anyone," and nothing can keep you from your 10 but your own thinking.

What happens when you ask this question? You create the G.A.P. of Opportunity. Your RAS will open up and find the information you need to keep your 10, and scotoma out the information that would take it away. Now if you see that your tire is flat, you're going to say, "I want to keep my 10 no matter what." Ask yourself, "How do I make this a part of my 10?" Find a way to enjoy changing your flat. Are you going to let a tire—a inanimate object with no personality or attitude—give *you* a bad evening?

Change your thinking, and you'll change your life. I've had people in my seminars come back the following day and share amazing stories of what happened when they lived out a 10 evening. Here's one story I'd like to share.

I was doing a seminar for a company that was mandatory for all employees. One gentleman, a technician, made it obvious—by several comments and body language—that he didn't want to be there. On the first day, I gave the group the exercise about having a 10 evening, and the next morning, I asked them about the experience. The technician was the first person to raise his hand.

He began by saying, "Last night I did your stupid exercise… ." Remember, I'd made my mind up about him before I met him. I was locked on to the idea that this guy was brilliant, awesome, forgiving, and fun-loving. But it's a struggle, right? He was doing everything he could to make me change my attitude about him, or in other words affect my 10.

Then, he continued: "Well, I went home, and all I wanted to do was to watch a rerun of "ER" on TV. So when the program was about to start, I went into the den and found my fifteen-year-old watching some stupid show! I was getting ready to throw him out of the room so I could watch "ER," and I thought about your stupid exercise. Something inside of me said, "Wait a minute!"

Suddenly, the technician's tone changed. He went from sarcasm to sincerity. "I walked into the room and sat down. Before I could open my mouth, my son said, 'Dad, do you want me to change the channel and leave?'

"It dawned on me that all I had to do was enter a room, and my son would take off. I remembered the exercise, so I said, 'No. Why don't you go ahead and watch whatever you want?' Deep down, I must admit, I was still thinking, 'Man, I'm not going to get to watch "ER!" What am I doing?' I looked down, and while I was staring at the floor and being mad at you, Larry, the room suddenly became quiet. My son had turned off the television. I looked up. My son said, "Dad, do you think we could just talk?"

You could've heard a pin drop in the room at that moment.

The technician added, "Larry, it's the first time in three years my son and I have had a conversation. My night last night was a 15 on a scale of one to 10. I see now what you're talking about. If I hadn't done the exercise, I would've let him leave the room, and I would have watched another rerun."

How much of the life that's happening right in front of us are we missing because we're too busy getting somewhere? You can have a 10 tonight *no matter what*. It's your choice. Why not have one from here on out?

A Final Note

We've reached an important midpoint in the L.I.F.E. lessons. We're now moving beyond the importance of having a vision and the role that thinking plays in your life, and on to ways to begin taking the proper actions to accomplish your visions. As you learned earlier, a key element of vision accomplishment is the S.T.E.P.S. formula. Now you will begin the process necessary to see your vision, truly emotionalize it, and make it seem so real that you'll feel as if you've already accomplished it. Then, you'll be well on your way to getting a vision and living it.

Lesson 5
Reflection Questions

Where have you used the S.T.E.P.S. formula in your past to form a new vision, and where are you using it currently?

Since you can use the S.T.E.P.S. formula to get what you *don't* want, as well as what you do, what can you do now to ensure that you only use it in a positive fashion?

What changes would take place in your work or personal life by deciding to have a 10 everyday?

How does the 10 exercise affect your RAS?

How can the 10 exercise facilitate your ability to accomplish your vision?

I take away the following insight from this lesson …

I intend to use it first in the areas of …

Because …

118

List the behaviors you would like to change or visions you would like to accomplish:

Lesson 6: Getting What You Want is as Easy as Getting Home

"Believe that you have it, and you have it."
— Erasmus, 16th Century

O nce you have established a vision, you can take one of two courses of action. You can contemplate (based on past experience) all of the most logical reasons why you *won't* be able to accomplish your vision, or you can contemplate (based on what's possible), all the reasons why you *can* accomplish the vision. The choice you make becomes the difference between mediocrity and excellence.

The greatest challenge you face in achieving or becoming what you want is not in the *building of the vision*, but in how you talk to yourself *about the obstacles that stand in your way.* You must first spend the appropriate amount of time defining the vision.

Can you see, feel, touch, taste, smell, and live the vision before you get there? If that sounds like a different strategy to vision accomplishment than you're used to, you need to pay close attention to this lesson. By now, you should understand the power of your Rox-Talk,™ and its role in the formation of your belief system. Just as the young accordion player developed a belief about his musical talent based on the perceptions of others and talked to himself about that information, you also govern your life with beliefs that were formed the same way. Vision alone won't make you successful. *You must act upon the vision.* Since beliefs govern performance, is there any value in learning how to create new beliefs that override old ones, resulting in enjoying a quality of life that may now be nothing more than a wish? In this lesson, you will find out how to do just that.

> The illusion is not that the vision is too grand. The illusion is believing that the obstacles exist.

What Happens When the Vision Is Created

What happens physiologically when we decide to change? Remember, whenever we begin something, we always begin right here, *right now*. Let's call the way things are right now in your life your *current reality*. Stand on a scale in your bathroom—current reality. Look in your savings or checking account—current reality. This difference between your current reality—the way things are now— and your vision—the way you want to them to be—creates tension. This type of tension isn't negative, by the way. In fact, you and I should look forward to tension and discontent. Why? Because tension is a motivating force to help move us from where we are now to where we want to be. *There is no growth without discontent.*

Let's look more closely at this decision to change. Imagine a person who wants to lose weight. This particular person is five feet, eight inches tall and weighs 250 pounds. He's let himself go. But he's finally reached the point where he wants to change.

"You know what? I am sick and tired of how I feel. I have no energy, and many good feelings I'd like to have about myself are gone! I want to weigh 150 pounds! I'm going to lose 100 pounds. 150 pounds would be ideal for me at this point!"

Is this a vision? Not yet. Right now, it's a goal. His goal to lose 100 pounds. This is a goal and not a vision because he is focused on what he doesn't want, and not on what he does want. He is only talking about what he wants to move away from (in this case, a lack of energy and 100 pounds).

He'll have a vision when he begins to describe all of the benefits of weighing 150 pounds. At that point, he's seeing what he wants to grow into. The moment that he decided what he wanted, however, he immediately created a difference— the difference between where he is now and where he wants to be. Thus, he has tension in his system, and his system will begin to look for ways to reduce or eliminate the tension.

As human beings, we constantly strive for balance and always move toward a tensionless state. We cannot maintain tension for very long without doing something about it. The vast majority of people take the shortest route to alleviate the tension: *they lower their vision.*

"Well, you know, I don't look too bad. Thank God for pleated pants. I'll only lose a few pounds to begin with and… ."

However you rationalize it, if you don't know any other way, you will attempt to rid your system of the tension. Remember when I called in sick at the Cliff House? I got rid of the tension about performing in front of others by lowering my vision (in fact, I lowered my vision to the point where I had *no* vision of myself as a successful musician). When this happens, you don't get what you want—you don't achieve your vision—but you also don't have the tension any longer.

To most people, not achieving a vision feels like failure. Do this often enough and you begin to label yourself a failure. As a result, your self-esteem plummets. Sometimes we don't let ourselves want, because then we don't have to fail or let ourselves down.

> Any time you give up on a vision, you lower your self-esteem.

This tension between current reality and vision can be very powerful. In fact, we often label this with words—for example, we might say that we're "under a lot of tension." We might call it discontent. We might call it anxiety. We might call it stress. It's easy to understand why people do this: they have been living in their current reality for quite a while—sometimes many, many years. They believe that their current reality is *fixed* and their vision is only *temporary*. Vision, they believe, can come and go.

To avoid falling into this trap regarding current reality and visions, what do we need to choose to believe?

> Current reality is not fixed; it's only temporary. The only thing that should be fixed is vision.

Here's another example I like to use in my seminars. Most of us believe that our current reality is fixed. It's like we have bungee cords strapped to our body, and these bungee cords are tied to a fixed thing—our current reality. As we move toward our vision, at first everything is fine. We move away from our current reality and see some progress. Soon, the bungee cords begin to tighten. Then they stretch. Finally, the strain is too much, and they snap us back to our current reality. We're back where we were before, but now our bungee cords are slack, and the tension has disappeared.

Take those bungee cords and attach them to your vision instead. Keep imagining how you want your life to be, and the next thing you know, you'll arrive at your vision. You'll think, "I didn't even have to work hard at it! This new reality goes against everything I have seen, heard, and tried...but at a deeper level, it supports everything that's right about myself!"

The Difference between Goals and Vision

Let's continue discussing the difference between goals and vision. This differentiation is critical to achieving prosperity.

A goal is one of many necessary steps to achieve a vision. A goal is "what" you need to do, and a vision is "why" you want to do it. Vision provides the motivation to accomplish the goal. When you don't know what your vision is, the goal can easily become a "have to."

Here's an example:

Goal: Have a party at your house.

Vision: Who you'll invite, what foods you'll serve, what games will be played, what time the guests will arrive, what the guests will wear, what the mood will be, and so on.

Let's say that you have a vision about this party. Since you have a vision, there are many goals you need to accomplish in order to pull off the vision—making phone calls, buying groceries, etc. No matter how exciting your vision is, the moment you ask someone else to help, he or she says, "Why?" *Whenever we ask others to participate in our vision, the goals we ask them to meet become "have tos," not "want tos," unless they share our vision.* In this mind-state, they will only do what they are asked, and nothing more, because it's your vision, not theirs. Since you created the vision for the party, you have no internal "push-back" on accomplishing the goals. *But if you haven't involved others in the creation of the vision, problems will arise.*

Many parents plan vacations based on what they think their children will enjoy. They often find themselves constantly yelling at the kids to shut up and stop fighting throughout the trip, and the journey becomes a nightmare. When parents involve children in the planning process by asking them what they would like to do on a vacation and select a destination together, the journey becomes as fun as the destination.

> Visions created by family or members of the organization are accomplished in *half the time* compared to those created by leadership or a single person.

The Power of Vision

If your vision is stronger than your current reality, you will be successful. What's more, if your vision is stronger than your current reality, you'll quickly realize that end results are much more important than the "how-tos." If your vision is strong enough, you'll know how to accomplish goals. The "hows" will create themselves.

Many people don't believe that vision accomplishment can be so easy. They get hung up on "how" they're going to accomplish the vision. The how doesn't matter; it will come of its own accord. Let me give you an example. You've worked all day at the office. It's five o'clock, and you're ready to go home. That's your vision. Your means of getting home—driving your car, taking a bus, or whatever—are your goals.

Let's say you're on your way home, and your tire blows out. Boom—you can't drive your car. Would you put a "For Sale" sign on your car and wander away? You wouldn't just give up and say, "That's it, I'm never getting home." Of course not. You'd have to come up with a new plan of *how to get home*, but you'd still make it home.

Let's say you change the tire, and just as you're back on the road, your engine suddenly blows up. Your car doesn't work. Are you still going to get home? Only if your vision is stronger than your current reality.

Here's an important point to remember: there is *no difference* between achieving any vision you have and our example of getting home at night after work. I know you might be thinking, "Wait a minute, Larry. I've been fine with what you've been saying up until now. But this, I'm not buying. Achieving a vision and getting home are very different."

When I ask people during my seminars how reaching a vision and getting home are different, some of the typical responses are:

- Home is my comfort zone; I'm familiar with it.

- I've been home before. I haven't achieved a particular vision before.

- I've experienced success with home.

- I know the way home.

- Home is physical: I can feel it and see it.

- There's no doubt that I'll get home.

- Home is more valuable than vision.

- It's easier to get home.

- I already know how to overcome the obstacles to get home.

There are usually others, and you may have some different ones, but that's a pretty good list. Now let me ask you this question: if not for these differences, would reaching your vision and getting home be the same thing? We could keep listing differences as you bring them up, but ultimately you'd agree that if it wasn't for the differences they are the same. Now this doesn't mean that you believe they're the same yet. I'm not worried about your belief yet. Let's just do a little logic lesson here. If not for these differences, would getting home and achieving a vision be the same? Yes.

These differences exist in the only place that matters, your mind, and nowhere else. When I have seen myself over and over and over again as a lean, keen, change-agent machine standing on a scale that reads 150, I have a Roxometer that believes I'm a lean, keen, change-agent machine. I feel light, effortless, and effervescent. I can play longer than my kids and I don't get winded on hikes. What happens when I visualize that over and over? The belief overpowers the old Roxometer, the one that said that I was overweight, slovenly, and low on energy.

When I have been to the "new me" over and over again in my mind, I become comfortable with this belief about myself. This means I'm in the *comfort zone.* This is extremely powerful when used in the right way. If it was suddenly time for you to go home, your belief would be that you're in no danger of *not* getting home, right? There's nothing that could prevent you from ultimately getting home. The how doesn't necessarily matter, does it? You might take your car. If your car breaks down, you might call a friend or family member. You might take a bus. But eventually, you'd arrive home. Why would you arrive home? Because home has *value.* Right? It's your sanctuary. Your family is there. It's where you relax.

Let's talk about vision again for a moment. We all agree that we've been home over and over again. If I have been home over and over in my mind, is that the same as physically being home before? Absolutely! I've been to my vision so many times in my mind that I'm acting according to my vision right now. My vision of home began in my mind. You didn't find yourself with this book in your hands without first telling yourself you were looking to bring more to your life. You found the book you were looking for, picked it up, and started reading it. You are living your vision now, even though you haven't finished the book yet.

The mind is a powerful thing. Imagine a company beginning a major change. The employees who have a vision of the company are going to have to change their thinking and begin living the new way, or the change is doomed from the beginning.

You must not only see your vision first, but also believe that you have already obtained it.

"I'll know I've achieved my vision when I arrive."

"How will you know?"

"Because I'll have all the evidence."

126

Wrong! Remember how the RAS works: *The vision comes first and* then *you see; you do not see the evidence first.* Avoid doing this backwards, trying to see the evidence and results first, and believing you have arrived.

Let's continue this point. People often tell me, "Well, Larry, home's a physical thing, and vision is just an idea." Remember, reality is how we see it, and reality causes us to take action. There's no doubt about my vision of home. Doubt occurs at the same moment I begin to imagine what will be necessary to accomplish the vision. It forms when we think about the how. Remember, what's the first thing that everybody starts to think about the moment that they begin to think of their vision? The *how.* That's where doubt lies. This, more than anything else, is why people don't achieve their vision—they automatically begin to focus on the *how* and automatically create doubt in their minds. *You create the doubt, which more often than not stops you from achieving your vision.*

Why the "How" Can Create Doubt

Let's return to the exercise example for a moment to explore why it's so dangerous to think about the "how" at the same time you create your vision. If I currently weigh 250 pounds and want to weigh 150 pounds, I'll have to change my diet. Let's examine why diets fail, and why most people don't accomplish everything they want.

Albert Bandura, a research psychologist, once said, "You and I will not allow ourselves to want that which we don't think we can pull off." *The following is probably the most important information you will receive about vision accomplishment.*

Of course, I have current eating *habits*—what I eat, when I eat, and how much I eat—that I will have to change. We all do. Habits are extremely powerful, because they come from the subconscious. Do these powerful habits support 250 pounds, or 150 pounds? In Lesson 4, we learned that we are wired to maintain sanity, and sanity is our currently dominant self-image. This is not something that we pay attention to consciously. Consciously, I want to weigh 150 pounds, but subconsciously I have something else going on.

Exercise is the next step. Of course, I have many *attitudes* about exercise. Remember, attitudes affect performance 100 percent. Are you beginning to see why change can be so difficult for people who don't know how they think?

Here's another wrinkle: I have many *expectations* about how successful my attempt to lose weight will be. My conscious mind is saying, "I want to weigh 150 pounds," but my subconscious knows I weigh 250 pounds. My subconscious mind, in fact, saying, "You weigh 250 pounds. The scale says so and your refrigerator is backing it up. Your closet is filled with clothes that fit a person who weighs 250 pounds. Who do you think you're kidding?" Changing my subconscious is the key, because subconscious habits, attitudes, and expectations equal one big belief, and belief drives behavior. Another word for belief is self-image, and another word for self-image is Roxometer.

If you don't first change your self-image, the obstacles along the way will always appear bigger than your vision. Objects in the mirror are never as big as they appear.

Spending the appropriate amount of time defining the vision instead of *trying to figure out how to achieve it* will improve your likelihood of reaching the vision by tenfold.

> Stay away from the "how" when you are establishing your the vision, because if the "how" was effective, you'd already be at your vision. You have an attitude about the "how."

The Vision's Power Will Create the How

If you accept a vision and participate in identifying its value, amazing creative processes begin. It's phenomenal! The vision may be the same one you've always had, but now there's a new sense of attitude and purpose behind it. You might even do the same things you've always done that once prevented you from achieving the vision—but now you don't care, because you see both the vision and its value!

"But exercise is work."

"I don't care! Not to me!"

With vision, you're not focusing on the exercising; you're focusing on *what you've become* by *doing the exercising*. The vast majority of people just focus on the exercise. "Oh, this is hard! How far have I run? I don't know if I can go any farther!" Instead, focus on your vision. "My vision is to be a lean, keen, 150-pound change-agent machine, and in order to become one, I get to run one more block!" When you focus on the vision, in many cases old "have tos" now become "want tos."

Let's discuss another "difference" between getting home and achieving a vision. You might say that a vision isn't as valuable as getting home, but I don't buy that. Vision is way more valuable than current reality, because why would you create a want that doesn't have value?

One person suggested that the difference between getting home and realizing a vision is that people are willing to do whatever it takes to get home. Would you *not* do whatever it took to achieve what you wanted to achieve, if all you had to do was imagine what you wanted and let the "how" automatically fall into place? Of

128

course you would. Instead, you've been taught to think, "What's the plan? What's the process?"

Most people never consider that they won't get home. But that's not true when it comes to vision. We often see ourselves failing. Not good. Consider pilots: they don't practice crashing. They don't say, "Hey, let's go crash that plane. I know it costs a lot of money, but it's the only way to learn." Pilots practice what to do in order to *prevent* crashes. They use flight simulators to practice preventing crashes.

Your simulator is your imagination. Don't practice worry. Don't practice falling short. Don't practice concern. Practice the way you want your life to be, and act that way starting *right now*. "Get a vision and live it."™ *Right now!*

Getting home is a powerful example of achieving vision, but here's an even better one. Why don't people crawl around like babies? People learn to walk because they see other people doing it. Walking has advantages. You can reach cookies. You can move around faster.

Does learning to walk happen easily? No, in fact, it can be quite painful. Imagine a one-year-old who's just gotten six stitches in her forehead because she fell while trying to walk. The moment she's put back down on the floor, she'll try to walk again. If adults experienced the same kind of risk every time they tried to walk, they'd have a much different attitude. "Walking is dangerous! I don't think I'm going to do that anymore. I could get killed. I'm going to stick to crawling."

Why don't kids give up? The answer is as profound as it is simple: A child doesn't know any better. That's amazing! *Giving up is a learned behavior.* We weren't born knowing how to give up. Did you get that? We weren't born knowing how to give up. We have to learn to give up, and some of us have become pretty good at it, too. Remember how many "nos" we heard as youngsters? Some of us are experts at giving up. "I tried. I really did, but it wasn't meant to be. Maybe I'll try something else. This isn't for me. You know, I've never been very good at it."

Some of us have become adults, which to me is little more than an abbreviation for "a dull thinker." We're very mature now. What if your boss at work came up to you and said, "We work in a very serious business here. There are quotas to meet and meetings to attend. I've noticed that you've been late to the last three meetings. What's wrong with you?" How motivated would you be at that particular moment? Not very. Everything's too serious. It's a *meeting* we're talking about. When leaders start having fun and getting a kick out of themselves, instead of kicking others, productivity soars.

As a leader, the more control you give up, the more control you have. It's exactly the opposite of what most leaders think. "I've got to have control! I've got to be tough," they think. Can you grow people that way? Definitely not.

Chaos can be a frightening thing, so there must be some order. Prosperity occurs when you know that to grow a company, you must first grow its people. Leaders and their people must develop *parameters*, which are valued principles and the purpose behind their organizational lives. As long as people have fun living within those parameters and know their purpose, abundance is the by-product.

The most important points to remember are:

1. You must be as certain that you will obtain your vision as you are certain that you will get home each night after work.

2. Almost no one succeeds at something the first time. It might take two or three times, or 300 or 400 times, but you must continue, no matter what.

3. The strength of your vision determines your success, not your intelligence or the quality of your plan.

A Final Note

Lesson 6 has continued to build on the foundation for achieving what you want in life. You've also learned about some of the obstacles you'll encounter along the way. You will run into stress when your vision is different from your current reality. You will occasionally fail. But if you have a vision that's compelling and that you believe you have already obtained, you will succeed beyond your wildest dreams, no matter the obstacles.

You must also avoid, as much as possible, worrying about "how" you will obtain your visions. The "how" will come when you believe. Here's an important statement to remember:

> I have no right to work on the "how" until I can touch, taste, feel, smell, see, hear, emotionalize, and own the vision.

Why is this true? Because once you own the vision, you suddenly begin to see everything necessary to pull it off all around you. Once again, the miraculous RAS locks on to the information necessary to pulling off whatever you have determined is significant—your vision.

Lesson 6
Reflection Questions

Think of an activity or situation that you would like to improve. What obstacles do you need to overcome to improve in this area?

Why can the "how" interfere with the size of the vision?

When does the "how" get created?

When you next begin to feel tension at home or work, for example, what can you do to reduce it based on what you've learned so far about the L.I.F.E. lessons?

How will the "going home" example help you the next time you run into obstacles as you attempt to achieve your vision?

I take away the following insight from this lesson ...

I intend to use it first in the areas of ...

Because …

_____

_____

_____

_____

_____

List the behaviors you would like to change or visions you would like to accomplish:

_____

_____

_____

_____

_____

_____

_____

_____

Lesson 7: Vision Accomplishment Is Simply Becoming Your New Picture

"You must be the change you wish to see in the world." — Mahatma Gandhi

You are beginning to understand the essential point of your existence: *Life doesn't get any better than it is **right now***. You were born with the equipment necessary to accomplish whatever you choose. You are the most powerful force on this planet. With the proper vision, you can change anything about yourself that may be holding you back.

Now, ask yourself this question: "Are there any areas in my life where changing an old habit, attitude, belief, or expectation would enhance the quality of this very precious and special life that I have?" You have spent many years talking to yourself about what you *don't* like and what you *wish* would change. You have recently learned that any time you talk to yourself about anything, you continue to reinforce that picture, whether it's what you want or not. So how do you change?

That's the focus of Lesson 7—how to make changes in your life. When I say changes, I mean accomplishing your visions.

This is where the L.I.F.E. lessons become really exciting. You are about to enter into the most exciting journey of your life—becoming the person you've always dreamed of being and having the things in life you've always wanted. Let's put this into perspective, however, by recalling this quote from Shakespeare: "We are but actors on the stage of life." Who is the star of your play? Who is in every single scene? You've been playing "you" for so long that you've got the part memorized. No matter what the situation, you automatically handle it, day in and day out, whether it's good for you or not.

What would you do if you were given the opportunity to star in a play where the lead is the you you've always wanted to be? What would you do with the old script? You wouldn't throw it away; instead, you'd simply change the parts that don't match the new you. That's what this lesson is all about—rewriting the new you properly and imprinting it, so you automatically and effortlessly become your new end results in all the areas you choose.

Vision accomplishment is simply becoming your new picture. As Cicero said, "Let us not go over the old grounds; let us rather prepare for what is to come." Let's now move beyond the current you to the life and person that you want to become.

Vision Statements

One of the primary things necessary to accomplish any vision is a *vision statement*. What is a formal vision statement?

> A vision statement is a statement of fact or belief accepted literally by your subconscious. It is a new ROX, which creates a new Roxometer.™

You create a vision statement simply by writing it down. Now please don't freak out here. You might be thinking, "Oh, boy. Here comes the hard work." But that's not the case. Throughout this chapter, I'll prove to you that vision statements are simple and concise enough to fit on a three-by-five-inch index card. You'll create vision statements for various areas of your life, and you'll review the vision statements a minimum of two times a day—once in the morning, before you start your day, and once at night, before you go to sleep.

Please stay with me here. This won't suck up hours and hours of your time each day. If you have 15 vision statements, and each one takes 10 seconds to read, that's a total of 150 seconds—two and a half minutes! Can you spare two and a half minutes in the morning and two and a half minutes at night to transform your life? I'll bet you can.

Vision statements must concern something that you want to change in your life. Let me give you an example using one of my vision statements concerning my relationship with my son, Connor.

Connor was five, and I was 47. As you can imagine, five-year-olds and 47-year-olds have different expectations about proper behavior. I had a lot going on in my life. I was traveling for business much more than I wanted to be. I found myself acting uptight and impatient whenever I was with Connor, and I didn't like the way I was acting. Instead of focusing on what

I *didn't* want, I did what I've been sharing with you and asked the key question: *how do I want it to be?*

I answered that question with a vision statement designed to change that part of my life.

Here's the vision statement I created:

> I feel valued, loved, and inspired because
> I am calm and patient with Connor.

After I wrote this vision statement, believe me, I didn't know *how* I was going to be calm and patient with Connor, but that was okay—I now had a vision of what I wanted to become, so I knew the "how" would take care of it itself.

Shortly after I wrote the vision statement, I took a business trip that lasted almost two weeks. Even though I was gone, I reviewed the vision statement each morning and evening for the duration of my trip. I finally returned from my trip late one Friday night, and I had planned to spend the entire next day with Connor. It would be our day. Quality time, not quantity time. (I've found over time that if you're not careful, that idea can become a rationalization, and soon a reality.)

Remember, my challenge was that whenever Connor and I would get together to do something, I'd become uptight and impatient. The more I focused I became on this undesirable behavior, the more I kept dropping ROX into my negative bucket. That's why I wrote the vision statement.

So Saturday morning arrived, and I was ready to have fun with Connor. In fact, I had the whole day planned: we were going to go to an indoor play gym, have lunch together, and catch a movie. I was in total harmony with this plan, of course, because it was my plan—Connor would have fun no matter what.

Just as we were about to leave for our day, I remembered that there were a few things that I needed to buy at the grocery store for a dinner we were having the following evening. I'd run in, get the stuff, and get out. I really didn't want to take Connor with me to the store, because bringing him along would take much longer and he was prone to the "gimmies." I knew that he would pressure me to buy something, and I didn't want to get uptight and impatient with him.

"Connor, I'll be right back. I've got to go to the store first," I told him.

Connor looked up at me. "Dad, can I go to the store with you?"

It was a simple question. Was going to the store with Connor part of my plan for the day? No. But what was my vision? Spending the day with Connor. Be careful of your plans, because they can get in the way of having the time of your life *right now* and the fulfillment of your vision.

I was moving right into cognitive dissonance. I became uptight and impatient, exactly what I *didn't* want to be. But I recognized what I was doing. I said to Connor, "I'll make a deal with you, son. You can go along if you don't get the gimmies. I just want to get in and out of there."

Kids will look you right in the eye and lie to you. He said, "Okay, Dad! I won't." He wasn't really lying, of course. He was living in the now, and right then, in the kitchen, there was nothing that he wanted. So we hopped in the car and we were off to the store.

The shopping trip went better than I'd expected. I gathered the things that we needed and moved the cart toward the checkout stand. Suddenly, I found myself in the crosshairs of the danger zone—the toy section. Connor said, "Dad, can I get a toy?"

I reverted to the past. Immediately I locked and loaded. *We're in a hurry. We've got to get back to the plan so we can spend quality time together.* At least I did remember this day was for Connor, so I caught myself a little. Without trying, the new self-image of being calm and patient was starting to work, so I said, "Fine, Connor, you can get a toy, but hurry up!"

Connor said, "Okay, Dad. I will!"

As soon as that little guy said that, I just cracked. I realized at that moment that I'd been actlng uptight and impatient. This is exactly when cognitive dissonance kicks in. *You can't hold two conflicting thoughts ln your mind at the same time without creating disharmony.* I now had one foot on the dock (current reality) and one foot on the boat (vision). The dock was me being uptight and impatient, and the boat was me being calm and patient. I was confronted with a choice. At least I had that. If you don't create a vision, you've got no choice, and you simply react as you've been conditioned to react.

Remember, you don't have to plan the "how." I already had the day planned. But with a vision, I knew the "how" would take care of itself.

I immediately sat on the floor of the grocery store, looked at Connor, and said, "Connor, you take all the time you want."

Connor looked horrified. Why? Because he had gotten comfortable with his old dad. He didn't know how to deal with this new guy, so his mind was on full alert: "Something's wrong!" Nervously, he said, "I'll hurry, Dad!"

My tone didn't change. "No, Connor. Take all the time you want. I mean it."

He still didn't quite know how to handle this. He pointed to the toys and said, "Dad, which one can I get?" We had a house rule about toys—no weapons.

I said, "Connor, you can get any toy you want."

He looked at the toys, looked at me, looked at the toys again, and said, "Dad, I love you!" And then he grabbed a gun.

Connor was happy, and I felt good, too. He dropped the toy gun in the cart. I got up, wiped the dust off my pants, and we paid and left the store.

It's amazing what we can get caught up in. If I hadn't come to my senses right then, getting those groceries home would have been more important than spending that moment with Connor. What's more important? What really happened in that grocery store that day? I created a G.A.P. of Opportunity, didn't I? Do you know what else G.A.P. can stand for? Give A Present. I gave Connor a toy, any toy he wanted, but what I really gave him was priceless—my time. I made him feel important. *I gave Connor his moment in time.* Did I get anything in return? You bet! I felt better about myself, and Connor and I went on to have an awesome day. We were late for the movie, but who cares? Connor didn't care if we were late, and perhaps for the first time in my life, neither did I.

By the way, Connor held on to that toy gun for more than three years. He didn't hold up any convenience stores or shoot anyone, but I'm sure he kept it because it reminded him of our special moment.

Vision statements will help us "catch" ourselves from reacting to the old ways of thinking and doing, and allow us to now act the way we want things to be. Remember:

> If you don't create the new, you're stuck with the old.

When Something "Bugs" You

How does the process of picking the subject matter of your vision statements begin? Do people sit around saying, "My life is perfect now, but I'd really like this and this, too?" Not always. *You must first be discontent with the old before you are compelled enough to create the new.*

This takes some soul-searching on your part. It's simple, though. I want you to identify something that is bugging you in your life right now, something about which you could say, "If I fixed that, I'd feel better about my life." It could be a bad habit you've developed, a relationship you're in, or how you communicate or otherwise interact with a co-worker. The key is this: this must be a problem to you. It must be something that you want to change—not your spouse, not your significant other, not your boss or co-workers, and certainly not your parents. You.

Jot down what's bugging you on the top of page 141 so you can refer to it later. In reference to my dilemma with Connor, I would have written, "I'm uptight and impatient with Connor."

Once you have written down your challenge, select one of the growth areas from the list below that your challenge falls under and add it to line number 1. In my case, I would jot down "Children" on the first line.

Suggested Growth Areas

- Physical Health
- Children
- Marriage
- Community
- Attributes*

- Family
- Spouse
- Significant Other
- Mental Health

- Spiritual Life
- Recreation
- Retirement
- Friends

- Financial Health
- Education
- Social Life
- Vocation

* Attributes are qualities or characteristics that you would like to make a part of your core. You already possess these attributes, but you need to create vision statements for them so you can consciously make them part of your current behavior. Attributes include courage, honesty, faith, gentleness, unconditional listening, calm, grace, sense of humor, friendliness, and so on.

Does one thing that bugs you come immediately to mind? It should, unless you've become so used to it that it doesn't bother you any more.

As you move through the rest of this chapter and the L.I.F.E. lessons, I suggest that you seek to balance your life by selecting a minimum of six essential growth areas from this list for your vision statements. Jot down five more areas in which you feel you need to be doing well in order to have a well-balanced life. (You may circle them if you wish. It's your book!) But for now, let's focus on one area that you want to improve upon.

Six Essential Categories of My Life:

1. _____

2. _____

3. _____

4. _____

5. _____

6. _____

What's currently bugging me? My example would be: I'm uptight and impatient with Connor and feel like a bad dad. Be as specific as you can when stating what's bugging you.

Vision Statement Ingredients

The following "ingredients" are combined to create effective vision statements that will literally change the pictures within your subconscious, thus creating new Roxometers.

Personal Ownership

Personal simply means that the vision statement should be *about you*. You can't write a vision statement for someone else. "Read these twice a day, honey, and then we'll have an incredible relationship." Remember, others don't like to be told what to do. Any time we try to change someone, no matter how subtle we may be, our audience will be less than responsive. (The best change agent is to model, or act out, the behaviors you'd like to see in others. Remember Gandhi, "You must be the change you wish to see in this world.")

Your vision must be yours...not your spouse's, not your boss's, and not anyone else's. Thus, vision statements typically start with "I." Focus on yourself, and the changes you want to see, do, or become.

Lean

Remember, with the Roxometer you're dropping ROX into whatever category you're thinking about. By creating this new vision, you are attempting to literally change your thinking and change the configuration of brain cells in a specific area. Remember, too, that attitude dictates what you lean toward. Your brain doesn't follow directions, it follows words, so *lean* simply means *write about what you want, not what you don't want.*

Have you ever said to yourself, "I wish I hadn't done that..." or "I wish I hadn't said that...?" We all have, but the past isn't going to change. That type of thinking isn't going to change you either. In fact, by thinking those thoughts, you're continuing to affirm what you don't want.

Remember my vision statement about being with Connor. I didn't write, "I feel loved, valued, and inspired by Connor because I am no longer uptight and impatient." That would have neutralized my desires. I would have dropped a ROX in "loved, valued, and inspired," but at the same time, I also would have dropped a ROX in "uptight and impatient." I wouldn't drop any ROX in "calm and patient," which is the direction that I wanted to go in.

Being specific with your thoughts is essential, as they are the building blocks of habits and attitudes.

Completion

I think you'll find this ingredient interesting, even if you're aware of this point on some level in your mind. Most people believe the vision or goal will be accomplished later, at some future point. That's the trap: Later doesn't exist! You can't wrap your arms around later, because we only live *right now*. So *completion* simply means that you should write your vision statement as though you already possess what it is that you want to have or become. *Write your vision statement as though it's already done.*

Companies are famous for existing in the future, aren't they? We've seen organizations that have envisioned a million-dollar increase in net revenue, projected the increase over a two-year period, and developed all the quarterly plans necessary to achieve them. They've even broken the plans down into daily activities needed to accomplish the increase, and at the end of the two years, they manage to pull it off and achieve what they wanted to achieve. Other organizations act like they had the increase *now*, and pull off the same achievements in only six months.

The same is true in our personal lives. If you're going to get in shape tomorrow, you're in no danger of doing anything today. We live in the *today*. We don't live in the *tomorrow*. To prevent a future-focused vision when writing your vision statement, avoid any words that imply it hasn't already taken place.

The important point to remember is this: *you and I will only take action on those things that we are affirming now. Everything else can wait.* Relax, take a deep breath, and feel calm. You did what you did because you were thinking about it *right now*.

Accomplishment

This is where a lot of people fall short when it comes to writing a vision statement. They end up getting what they think about. Remember, you're always going to get what you're thinking about, so make sure you're thinking about what you want. Don't talk to yourself about the problem. Don't affirm it. *Accomplishment means write about what I've done, not about what I'm capable of doing.*

Here's a quick example. Hold a pencil out in front of you between your thumb and forefinger. Focus on the tip. Say the following statement out loud three times while focusing on the tip: "I can drop it. I can drop it. I can drop it."

Did you drop the pencil? No. You had the *potential* to drop the pencil, but you didn't drop it. There was one word in that statement that didn't allow you to take action—can. "Can" affirms an ability, but it doesn't create action. "I can be a nice person...I can get my degree...I can get in shape...I can use the information in this book." Of course you *can* do any of these things, but are you doing them *right now?* Affirm what you've become, not what you're capable of doing.

Not "I can." Instead, "I am!"

If you take action toward your vision, something will happen. (This "something" could be positive or negative, of course.) If you *think* about taking action, *nothing* happens!

I'm beginning to make you more aware of the ongoing conversation you are having with yourself in your head. If you want to be successful, there are certain words you should stop using.

Can	Will	Once I ...	Try
As soon as...	I hope to ...	Wish	Tomorrow
If	I should've ...	I could've ...	Later
I would've ...	Hope	When	Some day ...
Maybe	Soon	As long as ...	At least
Might	Can't	Never	I'm going to ...

Every one of these words can derail even the simplest vision.

- *As soon as* I get a raise, I'll open an IRA.

- *Once I* finish school, I'll start saving money.

- *When* my kids get older, I'll take them to a baseball game.

- *Once I* have the time, I'll take more time for what's important.

What's missing in these four statements? Nothing is happening *now!*

There are other words to avoid as well. If you absolutely want to confirm that you'll do nothing *right now* about your situation, use the word *tomorrow.* Of the 3,000 or so languages in the world today, less than 100 have a word for "tomorrow." (English, of course, is one of those 100 languages.) If you never said that word to yourself or another person again, you'd be amazed at what would happen to your behavior!

Here's another word to avoid: Try. Stop *trying* to do anything. Either do it or don't do it. "Try" suggests an element of doubt, of possible failure. Do you want to be the best salesperson in your store? Then do it! Do you want to write a novel that people will enjoy? Then do it! Do you want to be the best you can be? Let's get started.

Words are powerful factors in our successes. *We control our words, both the ones that we speak and the ones we think.* The only thing holding you back is the attitude about something or someone you developed along the way. And quite frankly, more than likely you didn't even select that attitude, someone else selected it for you.

Here's a story about how words negatively influenced me. In high school, I was the starting quarterback on the junior varsity team. I had a phenomenal completion ratio. I was short for a quarterback—I stood only five feet, eight inches. I couldn't stay in the pocket because I had trouble seeing over our huge linemen, but I rolled out a lot and did a lot of jump passes.

We steamrolled every team we played. We were undefeated, outscoring our opponents 90–3. Our team was awesome.

In my senior year, I joined the varsity team. I had always dreamed of playing for Norm Mayor, the very successful long-time coach. On the first day of practice, Mayor said to me, "Okay, Mr. Hot Dog. I've heard about what you've done on the JV team. I know you call yourself a quarterback. Let's see what you can do." (I remember this vividly because the emotions attached to our ROX are powerful.) I took the snap from the center, rolled out, tripped, and fell flat on my face. All I could hear was the coach blowing the whistle. Mayor said, "You call yourself a quarterback? You can't even run. My God, you think you're a *quarterback?* No one playing quarterback that way is going to play for me!"

I set a record at Lincoln High School for the most interceptions in a season that year because I didn't believe in myself. Every time I started to throw the ball, I'd think, "I wonder if Coach Mayor is right? Was I a fluke in JV?" My teammates would be wide open, and I'd throw it over their heads or watch it fall short. For years, I had dreams in which I saw receivers wide open and couldn't release the ball.

I know you're thinking. "Larry, you're such a wimp. Why weren't you a man about it? Why didn't you tell that coach, 'I'll show you!'?" Most people will never do that. Most people are taught to respect authority, so they say things like, "Oh, really? Okay, I'll do it your way." It wasn't the coach's fault. *I just didn't know that I didn't have to accept what he'd said.* Mayor was only doing what he thought was in the best interest of the team, and he was coaching as he had been coached.

The power of words is immense. You may have been taught "sticks and stones will break my bones, but words will never hurt me." Well, words will hurt you if you allow them to become a part of your subconscious.

Accomplishment means what you've done, not what you're capable of doing. Remember, there are no coincidences. You have more than one hundred billion neurons ready to assist you. Your RAS will let in the information, ideas, and people needed to make your vision a reality. You are ready to succeed *right now*. You will never be any more "ready" than you are at this moment in your life.

Standing Alone

Vision statements must be about a change in perspective toward yourself, not someone else. *Standing alone* simply means remembering that *there's no one else like you*. I wish someone had told this a long time ago, because I've let a lot of people push me around. It wasn't Mayor's fault that I wasn't being a better quarterback—I allowed that to happen. I allowed myself to say, "He's better than I am." For a long time, I was very angry with Mayor. I'd say to myself, "He's the reason I played so poorly." *I* was the reason.

Now is when we begin to talk about *accountability*. Every organization wants its people to be fully accountable. "If it's to be, it's up to me. It's not your fault that I'm not doing well—it's mine."

Being accountable is an attitude that most people don't want to take on. We believe that circumstances and other people bear the responsibility for our current situations, but that's not true. In fact, we shouldn't want to blame others, because when we blame we lose our power to grow and improve. We can't change others, and in most cases we can't even change the circumstances. If that is our frame of reference, we are powerless. But we can always change ourselves, and the way we deal with those events, and as we do we regain our power and expose more of our God-given excellence.

No one who picks up this book is a broken person. We're all world-class athletes. The difference between first and second place is often measured in hundredths of a second, but it's the difference between first and second. *Standing alone* simply means *not making comparisons*. Don't compare how you're doing based on how someone else is doing. You can't control others. You can only control yourself.

What will happen if you compare yourself to others? For one thing, you'll always come up short. There will always be someone who can run faster, sell more, or be funnier than you. What else will happen? You might become discouraged, and when you're discouraged, you'll almost certainly lose your desire and your energy. Then what'll happen? You'll coast. Many times, great people have joined a company with the vision to get hired, and nothing more.

This all gets back to vision—specifically, keeping your vision where it should be. Here's a good example of a misplaced vision. In 1971, the Miami Dolphins had an incredible season, reached the Super Bowl, and blew it. They stunk the place up!

After the game, Nick Buoniconti, a linebacker for the Dolphins, was asked, "Nick, what goal did you guys set at the beginning of the year?"

Buoniconti replied, "Get to the Super Bowl. Why do you ask?" Do you see a problem here? These are world-class athletes!

The reporter paused. "You mean you didn't set a goal to *win* the Super Bowl?"

Buoniconti put his head in hands. "My God, no! All we did was talk about getting there."

The Dolphins did learn from their mistake. The next year, 1972, they posted a perfect 14-0 record and went on to win Super Bowl VII. All it took was one little tweak in their vision.

Once you reach a goal that you've set, you lose drive and energy to do anything else but sustain that goal. This is how many people lose their passion. After a while, they stop achieving and just show up. "I'm here. What's today's project?" Drive and energy come from the vision. "Where there is no vision, the people perish," Proverbs 29:18.

If you don't visualize how you want your day to be, you'll just show up and see how it goes. High-performance people get up each morning and say, "Here's how I want the day to go...I want it to be a 10." Their RAS will open up to all the information necessary to make sure that when they put their heads on their pillows at night, they'll keep their 10s.

Isn't that what we're learning? We're learning to be proactive, and to avoid being reactive. Reaction is based on attitude, and proaction is based on vision. We're all more successful when we're proactive. If you have no choice other than to be reactive, you must make sure in advance that your reaction causes you to reach your vision. You're affirming how you want to be as if you're that way *right now*.

Remember, *standing alone* simply means not comparing yourself to others. No one is any better than you because no one is exactly like you, and you're no more important than anyone else. We are all in this together. It's not about being the best in the world, it's about being the best *for* the world.

Emotion Words

The size of the ROX we put in our buckets is determined by the emotion we attach to them. *So this ingredient simply means the more the emotion is attached to your vision statement, the faster the change will occur.* Whenever you are looking forward to something, you are much more likely to take action about it in the short-term. When you are looking backward, you'll always be planning to start tomorrow. Remind yourself of what you already know: Whenever you're excited about something, that emotion will drive you home. Nothing can stop an emotionally charged person.

When we imagine our visions, they should be filled with activity and movement. When I imagined myself with Connor on that Saturday, it wasn't a snapshot in time. It was filled with activity and movement. We don't think in snapshots. We think in moving pictures, which is how we should be thinking about our visions.

Some people have told me, "I'm not good at visualizing things. I can't create good mental images." Baloney! Everyone can imagine, which is all that visualization is. Don't take yourself out of the race by saying you're not good at visualizing. When I say "turtle," do you imagine a pink tiger? There is magic to imagining. Create a dream vision in your mind, and you'll take action toward the vision without any effort.

Precision

One of the biggest challenges of vision statements is the precision with which they are written. Most people are vague when it comes to creating a vision statement.

"I want more money." What's wrong with that, you might say? Well, what if I gave you a penny? That's more money than you had before.

The question you need to ask yourself in that case is this: "How much more money?" Remember, once you reach your vision, you lose all of your drive and energy except what's needed to maintain your new vision. Being specific allows the RAS to hone in on your vision like a heat-seeking missile. We are teleological by nature, which means we are prone to targets. If your vision or target is strong enough, you will use feedback to reach it, rather than using the feedback to talk yourself out of what you want. *Precision* is about answering the question *What's the target?* as finely as you can. Anything else is unacceptable.

Over the years, people have told me about the amazing transformations that occurred when they honed in on this point. One man wrote down a vision statement that included the amount of his ideal paycheck. Later, he came up to me and said, "Larry, this absolutely blew my mind! I did exactly what you said and it worked!" He showed me his vision card and the check. They were exactly the same—*to the penny!*

You draw to yourself that which you feel worthy of. That's why people often leave one bad relationship for another. All they do is change the other person; they don't change themselves. The vision statements we create draw us to the energy we need to change through the magic of the RAS. It opens us up to the "right" information.

Be specific. "My kids all love me." You can read that vision statement until you're blue in the face, but it won't change your children's love toward you.

Here's a way to make this specific:

> I feel valued, honored, and at peace because I spend
> thirty uninterrupted minutes doing (you choose the project)
> with each child a week.

This vision statement is specific, plus there is an action you can take to make it happen. Notice that I didn't mention anything about my children loving me for my efforts. Trying to do something so others will think differently about you, or give you something in return, will generally blow up in your face. The law of reciprocity works without you needing to manipulate it. It's similar to hoping that an apple you've thrown into the air will come down.  Gravity works, period. Remember, "What goes around, comes around." Just give them your love and the rest will take care of itself. Again, the key is to know *exactly* what it is that you want. It may be helpful to visualize a literal target. Once you've established your target, your RAS will open up to help you achieve what it is that you want to achieve.

Symmetry

It's essential that as you grow in your life, you do so in a balanced way. That's what I mean by symmetry. No single area of your life should overpower all the others.

I once had a client in Florida who wanted to double his annual income, from $150,000 to $300,000 a year. He worked like crazy and his income began to climb, but he was out of balance in the other areas of his life. His work overshadowed everything else. His wife divorced him, and that didn't get his attention. His poor relationships with his kids didn't get his attention. The only thing that finally got his attention that his vision, and therefore his life, was out of balance were the paddles on his chest that jump-started his heart. The stress of his life had led him to have a heart attack. OOPS—he'd never set a priority to work out.

Study the suggested growth areas, which we've discussed previously.

- Physical Health
- Family
- Spiritual Life
- Financial Health
- Children
- Spouse
- Recreation
- Education
- Marriage
- Significant Other
- Retirement
- Social Life
- Community
- Mental Health
- Friends
- Vocation
- Attributes* (see note on page 140)

As you move forward with taking action for each of your visions, make certain that each vision is in balance with your other visions.

The Ability to Imagine It

The ability to imagine it simply means that you must write a vision statement that's realistic. For example, a person who's fifty years old, five feet tall, and wants to be a starting guard in the National Basketball Association is bound to be disappointed. I don't care how hard this person works—it isn't going to happen.

Remember the phrase, "Out of sight, out of mind." If we know deep down that we can't achieve our vision, everything we're doing is a waste of time and energy. The key is simple: break your big, bodacious vision down into smaller, doable goals.

Let's use dieting again as an example. Suppose you weigh 250 pounds and you want to get to 150 pounds. That's a big jump that won't happen overnight. You should create a vision for 150 pounds and then create step goals for, say, 10-pound increments. That's very doable, right? After you've lost the first 10 pounds, set another goal to get you down to 230 pounds, and so on. Sometimes you have to take baby steps. That's fine, as long as you don't stop along the way toward achieving your ultimate vision.

As you mature in this process, you will become less concerned about whether your vision is imaginable or not. You will discover that it is enough to simply want it. I may never be a player in the NBA, but I can play basketball on the weekends, watch the NBA on TV, or buy season tickets to watch my local pro team. If I'm really serious about getting close to the action, I can save enough money to *buy* a pro basketball team.

The Vision Statement Workshop

Now that we've covered the basic ingredients to vision statements, let's move on to actually creating them. Here's a step-by-step process to help you create effective and inspiring vision statements. I'll use the Connor story as an example along the way.

1. Select a specific area of your life that you would like to change or improve and jot it down below. Refer to the suggested growth areas above listed on page 140.

   My example: Children

   Your growth area: _____

2. Write down how this looks or feels now—the current reality. Ask yourself, "What do I want to move away from?"

   My example: I'm uptight and impatient with Connor and feel like a bad dad.

   Your challenge: (page 141) _____

3. Next, ask yourself, "What would my life look or feel like if I didn't have this problem or challenge?" (Or ask: "If I did improve or grow, how would I describe myself?")

My example: I am calm and patient with Connor.

Your end result: _____

Let's pause here for a moment. Usually at this step a yellow "Caution!" light will begin going off in your mind, and the little voice inside your head will say something like, "How on earth do you think you're going to pull that off?" Don't worry about this voice right now. Don't worry about "how" you'll obtain what it is that you want to obtain or become the person you want to become. Simply focus on what it would look or feel like if you didn't have the problem or challenge. Instead of being uptight with Connor, I'd be calm. Instead of being impatient, I'd be patient. My first thought when I dreamed this vision statement was, "How am I going to do this with a little guy who has his own mind, who does a million different things to make me uptight and impatient?" I decided that I couldn't worry about that when I was making the vision statement, and I had to have faith that I would be able to do it. Could I have *planned* to sit down in the grocery store like I did? No. But I knew what outcome I wanted—to be calm and patient with Connor—and the "how" simply came to me.

4. Review your answer to number three and write down three words that describe how you will feel once your vision becomes a reality. To help you with this, I've created a list of clarifying words on the next page. You don't have to use those words; you can come up with any words you want. The key to selecting the right words is this: how do you want to feel? Some people say, "How do I know how I'm going to feel? I haven't arrived yet." My response is: If you did achieve your vision, how would you like to feel? What lights you up? What gets you so excited that you forget to eat, that you need less sleep? What would be a *"Yes!"* for you? Pick three words. You don't have to limit yourself to only three, of course, but select a minimum of three so you'll invest a lot of emotion in it.

Remember, the more the emotion, the faster the change, so get the juices flowing.

My example: Valued, loved, and inspired.

Your clarifying words: _____

150

Clarifiers

Accomplish
Active
Admire
Adorable
Adventurous
Affectionate
Alert
Amazing
Ambitious
Articulate
Aspiring
Assertive
Attentive
Beautiful
Beloved
Blessed
Blissful
Brave
Bright
Brilliant
Calm
Caring
Charming
Cheerful
Clear
Clever
Colorful
Comfortable
Compassionate
Competent
Complimentary
Composed
Concise
Confident
Conscientious
Considerate
Cooperative
Courteous
Creative
Dazzling
Decisive
Delightful
Dependable
Determined
Dignified

Dynamic
Easy
Effective
Effervescent
Effortless
Electric
Elegant
Eloquent
Embrace
Encouraging
Endearing
Energetic
Enjoyable
Enlightened
Enterprising
Enthusiastic
Exciting
Expectant
Expressive
Faithful
Fantastic
Fascinating
Festive
Flexible
Fluent
Forgiving
Fresh
Friendly
Frugal
Fun
Gallant
Generous
Gentle
Genuine
Gifted
Giving
Glorious
Graceful
Gracious
Growing
Happy
Harmonious
Healthy
Hearty
Helpful

Honest
Honorable
Hospitable
Humble
Humorous
Illustrious
Immense
Impeccable
Impressive
Independent
Individualistic
Industrious
Influential
Ingenious
Innovative
Inspiring
Inspirational
Intellectual
Intelligent
Intense
Intentional
Intuitive
Inventive
Joyous
Jubilant
Just
Kind
Knowing
Knowledgeable
Lively
Lovable
Loving
Loyal
Luminous
Magnetic
Meaningful
Modest
Moral
Motivated
Natural
Noble
Nourishing
Outstanding
Passionate
Patient

Peaceful
Perceptive
Pleasurable
Polite
Positive
Powerful
Precise
Prepared
Prestigious
Principled
Productive
Professional
Proficient
Progressive
Prosperous
Punctual
Purposeful
Quick
Quotable
Radiant
Rational
Receptive
Refreshing
Relaxed
Reliable
Reputable
Resourceful
Respectful
Rich
Scholarly
Seeking
Selective
Self-confident
Self-contained
Self-reliant
Sensational
Sensitive
Sentimental
Sharing
Significant
Sincere
Skillful
Smooth
Spectacular
Spirited

Spiritual
Spontaneous
Steadfast
Strong
Stunning
Sturdy
Successful
Supportive
Swift
Systematic
Tactful
Tender
Terrific
Thankful
Thorough
Thriving
Tranquil
Treasured
Thoughtful
Triumphant
True
Trusted
Trustworthy
Truthful
Understanding
Uplifting
Valuable
Venturesome
Vibrant
Victorious
Virtuous
Visionary
Vital
Vivacious
Vivid
Warm
Welcome
Well
Wholesome
Winning
Wonderful
Worthwhile
Zestful

5. Describe the "new you" by using the vision statement ingredients. Here's a simple format to write your vision statements. Imagine that you're walking down the street, and off in the distance, you see an old friend you haven't seen in years. This friend walks up to you and says; "You look fantastic, what's different about you?" You'd say (using my example):

"I feel (step 4) valued, loved, and inspired because I (step 3) am calm and patient with Connor."

Your vision statement: "I feel _____, _____, and _____ because I _____

6. Next, check for vision harmony. To confirm that your vision aligns with your life, ask yourself how each of the following areas will be positively impacted once you achieve your vision. If you find an area of your life that won't be positively impacted by the change in you, reconsider your vision. The value of this checklist is in finding out what kind of impact the change will have on your life *before* you make the change. Typically people make a change and then they find out whether it was a good idea or not.

___Family	___Social Life	___Recreation
___Physical Health	___Spiritual Life	___Vocation
___Mental Health	___Financial Health	___Friends

My example: Now that I'm calm and patient with Connor, my family finds me fun and exciting to be with because of my patience. Our social life is growing, in part because of my relaxed and confident manner. I enjoy recreation with a focused mind because I'm focused at home. Now that I am calm and patient, my blood pressure and total physical health are in excellent condition. I feel at peace with my spiritual life and enjoy my resurgence of energy, which also benefits those I come in contact with. My vocation has risen to a new level of success due to my balance and sense of purpose. My mental health is positive and effective due to my calm and patient response to life's events. I am blessed with good financial health because I seek endless opportunities to give of myself. My many friends and I enjoy sharing our experiences because we value each other's uniqueness and look forward to our next great adventure.

The additional benefits to imagining the positive impact of your vision statement on the many facets of your life is that ROX get dropped into each category as you visualize and feel the emotional high of a balanced life.

7. Now test for imprinting clarity by reading your vision statement, picturing a specific behavior, and asking yourself what you experience in the following areas:

___seeing	___hearing	___feeling emotions
___touching	___smelling	___doing
___colors	___tasting	

My example: I <u>see</u> Connor having fun sharing with me as I drink it all in through my calm nature. I <u>hear</u> him telling me about his latest adventure while I hang on his every word. I feel love and warmth as <u>emotion</u> wells up in my heart and eyes from being with him. His hug is tight and his <u>touch</u> is light as he directs me towards the playground. I <u>smell</u> the cut grass and his sweet fragrant hair as we roll in the lawn. (And so on.)

Remember, the more vivid the vision statement and the more emotion it creates, the bigger the ROX. The bigger the ROX, the faster the change.

8. As a last step, write your completed vision statement on a three-by-five-inch index card.

> My example:
> I feel valued, loved, and inspired because
> I am calm and patient with Connor.

Vision Statement Reminders

Here are several key points to remember about vision statements:

- *Believe that it is now.* Don't use a single word that states or even implies that the vision you want to obtain hasn't already happened. The shortest distance between two points is not a straight line. It is a leap of faith. You must first believe.

- *Keep your visions to yourself.* I suggest that you don't share your vision statements with your spouse, your significant other, or even your friends. Why? Because then your vision becomes a "have to," rather than a "want to." Shared visions create expectations, and expectations create—consciously or unconsciously—pressure or tension to produce. It may make yourself second-guess your actions, question whether or not you are "living your vision," and create push-back in your mind.

- *Focus on **your** life, not the lives of others*. We've discussed this previously, but it bears repeating: You can't change others. You can only change yourself. Do you want a better relationship with another person? Focus on what **you** can do to improve that relationship.

- *Focus on what you want to change in your life*. The emphasis should be on what you want, not what others want for you. If you can't create a compelling reason to do something, don't do it!

- *Use experiential imagery*. In other words, see the vision through your own eyes. Make it so real in your mind that you can't help believing that you've already achieved your vision. What do you see, now that the vision is a reality?

- *Start small*. Develop six to 12 vision statements to begin with. Any more than that, and you may feel overwhelmed. Later, as you become more familiar and comfortable with living with vision statements, you can add more.

- *Review your vision statements at least twice a day*. I suggest you do so in the morning, right after you wake up, and at night, immediately before you go to sleep. Don't rush it. Take a minimum of 10 seconds to really imprint each vision statement in your mind.

- *Hop on the scale*. Check your current reality frequently. As you begin to use vision statements, your life will change; in fact, things will probably change quite quickly. You'll want to adjust to these changes, so it's important to review your current reality on an ongoing basis. Remember, there is no growth without discontent. You create the discontent by frequently checking out current reality as you live your exciting and inspiring vision.

- *Be prepared to achieve your visions*. Once you arrive at a goal or vision that you've set, be prepared momentarily to lose some drive and energy. This is natural; remember, the body and mind will naturally move toward atrophy if not properly motivated. What can you do if this is the case? *It's essential to enjoy your victory as much as it is essential for your personal growth to start a new game. So...create a new vision for this area of your life.*

Vision Statement Observations

As you begin to use vision statements, you must be aware of several potential challenges. For some people, you must first rebuild your self-esteem, and by that I mean that you must accept the fact that you can have and become what you want. Sometimes, receiving "too much, too soon" conflicts with our current reality—our current vision of ourselves. In these instances, we shrink back and contract. Accept the fact that you can grow beyond your wildest dreams. You can have the life you want, and you deserve everything that you want.

154

Always remember to avoid the trap of comparing yourself to others. We've discussed this before, but it's an important point to review. What if, for example, one of your visions is to be the number one salesperson at your organization? Currently you're number two, but you want to surpass Stan, who's been number one for the last five years. You work and work and work, and one day you learn that Stan won the lottery and resigned. Now you are the number one salesperson, but how do you feel about that?

Our culture creates enough comparisons to last us a lifetime. Each year, billions of dollars are spent on commercials that tell consumers what they should look like, smell like, and even feel like. Why get caught up in this if you don't have to? Your growth is a very personal and serious matter. You have chosen to leave behind what you have become because your current reality isn't bringing you the joy you want out of life. If you must compare, compare where you are now to where you want to be, not to where you think you should be or where you've been. Grow because it's *your* idea, not someone else's, and stay away from acquiring other people's opinions. I'd rather have people comment on the positive change they've seen in me instead of hearing about why they think I *can't* change, or why I *don't deserve* to have whatever it is I want.

S.T.E.P.S.^{sm} to Creating Your Life

Now that we have a handle on creating vision statements, let's move on to defining specific vision statements in specific areas of our lives. I call this process the S.T.E.P.S. needed to create your life. During this process, it's important to address obstacles you'll encounter when moving toward vision statements.

Step 1. Balance your life by selecting a minimum of six essential growth areas from the list below. You don't have to limit yourself to six, but use at least that many.

Suggested Growth Areas

• Physical Health	• Family	• Spiritual Life	• Financial Health
• Children	• Spouse	• Recreation	• Education
• Marriage	• Significant Other	• Retirement	• Social Life
• Community	• Mental Health	• Friends	• Vocation
• Attributes* (see note on page 140)			

Step 2: Select one area you want to change and then describe your current reality. Then create a vision statement using the steps on pages 149–153.

Step 3: Write down your vision statement in the area indicated on the chart entitled "My Vision Statements" on page 158.

Step 4: You have now determined both your starting point (current reality) and your destination (your vision). Should you confront an obstacle along the way to your vision, list it and then create a new vision statement by asking yourself this question: "What would my life look and feel like if I didn't have this challenge?"

Step 5: Continue this process for the rest of your selected growth areas.

Step 6: Transfer your vision statements on page 158 to three-by-five-inch cards, one statement per card. Review these at least twice daily—once in the morning and just before you fall asleep.

Bandura

No vision can be accomplished if you don't believe that you deserve to have or become the vision. You may remember that I mentioned the Canadian psychologist Albert Bandura, who teaches at Stanford University. Bandura specializes in *self-efficacy,* which is the belief in oneself that a person can cause, bring about, or make something happen. Bandura has studied thousands of individuals in an attempt to discover how much our past influences our future, and his findings reveal that in general, humans won't allow themselves to want what they don't think they can make happen.

We've all experienced this, haven't we? Perhaps you want to live in a more expensive home, but you don't think you can afford it. You probably won't even try to get a loan for that more expensive home, or take the steps necessary to change your economic circumstances. But our brains have proven time and time again that if we believe it, we can achieve it.

Building Self-Esteem One ROX at a Time

This all gets back to self-esteem. When you look at your past, you are always looking backwards. That can lower self-esteem. Instead, build your self-esteem. The next time something positive happens to you, don't pass through it too quickly. Allow yourself the opportunity to go, "Wow! That was really nice! I did that!" instead of saying, "Shucks, it was nothing. I couldn't have done it without my team." You need to take some of the credit. If you also want to give some credit to the team, great—do so. If you want to credit God, do that, too. But according to Bandura, you also need to take some of the credit.

You need to take some of the credit because as you are learning, when you replay the compliment or victory in your mind, it's as if it's happening to you again. Every time you think about it, you drop another ROX in the positive bucket. So next time you experience a victory, after you've thanked God and all of your friends, remember to also say "thank you" to yourself and tell yourself what a great job you did. If you don't raise your own self-esteem, who will? Don't discount your victories, large or small. When you discount a victory, a ROX gets dropped in your old opinion of yourself, rather than in the new one. In your mind, it's as if the event never actually happened.

Remember to do the world one favor, though: Keep your ROX to yourself. Stay away from "Yeah, I was great, wasn't I?" out loud. Others will classify that statement as arrogant, not confident.

A Final Note

What determines success in life? The power of your visions. If you don't have a new picture, you must keep responding to the old pictures. Now you have both the necessary ingredients and a simple way to create compelling, life-changing vision statements. Believe me, as you change your perception of self, your life will change, and that's a good thing. Too many people are afraid of change, and afraid of changing. Be a work in progress. Always be evolving into someone you were intended to be when you came into this thing called life. Allow yourself to become the person you want to be.

Remember that it's extremely easy to fall back to how things have always been. It's up to you to continue the process.

And what about the obstacles in the way? They'll be there; I'll guarantee you that. The power of the vision eliminates the hardships. Great salespeople are a good example of this. Most of them have to make cold calls to support their work. One survey revealed that 95 percent of salespeople don't like to use the phone. So why do they spend so much time and energy on the phone? They have a strong and compelling vision, and while they don't necessarily like the *how*, they *love* the results.

Be a work in progress. Believe that you deserve all that you want. Create vision statements that get you excited and compel you to take action. Remember: *Get a vision and live it!*

My Vision Statements

I feel _____ , _____ ,

and _____ because I _____

_____

_____

_____

I feel _____ , _____ ,

and _____ because I _____

_____

_____

_____

I feel _____ , _____ ,

and _____ because I _____

_____

_____

_____

I feel _____ , _____ ,

and _____ because I _____

_____

_____

_____

I feel _____ , _____ ,

and _____ because I _____

_____

_____

_____

I feel _____ , _____ ,

and _____ because I _____

_____

_____

_____

Lesson 7
Reflection Questions

Why should you write and read vision statements if you're interested in growing?

Why is it important to focus on *what* you want rather than *how* you're going to get it?

What should you do the next time you confront an obstacle?

How can you raise your own self-esteem, and why is it so necessary to do so?

How can you keep your vision stronger than your current reality? In your opinion, what is the most essential ingredient of a vision statement?

I take away the following insight from this lesson …

I intend to use it first in the areas of …

Because …

_____

_____

_____

_____

_____

List the behaviors you would like to change or visions you would like to accomplish:

_____

_____

_____

_____

_____

_____

_____

_____

_____

Lesson 8: Getting the Most Out of Life, *Right Now!*

" If one advances confidently in the direction of his dreams, and endeavors to live the life which he has imagined, he will meet with a success unexpected in common hours."
— Henry David Thoreau (1817–1862)

In this lesson, you will move beyond creating vision statements and go on to *living the change!* The Thoreau quote above is one of my favorites. If you dare to create your own visions, and dare to live it as though you've already accomplished them, then you will truly be getting twice the results in half the time with twice the fun!

Now, one of the biggest challenges you'll face in developing excellence is not what's "out there" in the world, but what's going on in your mind. *Your perception is always stronger than what you are perceiving.* In other words, what's happened to us isn't nearly as significant as how we talk to ourselves about that experience.

We've learned a great deal in the last few lessons about who we are, how we got that way, and how to go about changing if we choose to. We've also learned that if we don't change the old script, we can't respond to the new one. Next, we are going to move into the L.I.F.E. lessons where we learn to *live the change.* This lesson not only shares information about how to talk to yourself to enhance performance building self-image, but also about how to correct yourself or others while raising self-esteem. Your success or failure in life will depend not only on your ability to metaphorically fix your bike in the garage, which is intellectual, but more importantly your ability to fix your bike while you're riding it, which is experiential.

Rox-Talk™ Rehearsal

Have you ever heard of the "sure-enough" principle? How about the term "self-fulfilling prophecy?" If you expect a bad day, sure enough, you'll have a bad day. Think about everything you've learned from this book up to this point. Attitude is certainly one of the most powerful forces on this planet, isn't it? We *can* learn to control our thoughts, and when we can control our thoughts, our actions will follow, and those actions will lead to positive change.

The way we control our thoughts is called our Rox-Talk. Rox-Talk is that little voice you hear in your mind. The Rox-Talk Rehearsal process clearly explains how you should prepare for each moment, and if you don't like the outcome, how to prepare for, and adapt to, the next moment.

I specifically used the word "rehearsal," because that's exactly what you're doing. Your thinking is preparing you for the moment. There's an axiom that says, "Success happens when preparation meets opportunity." You must constantly prepare yourself to maximize every single opportunity.

Before we go on, let me state another axiom I'm certain you've heard before. "Opportunity knocks but once." Don't believe it for a minute. There are opportunities all around you. The problem is not a lack of opportunities. You're too busy to see or hear them because you aren't controlling your Rox-Talk—your Rox-Talk is controlling you.

Rox-Talk rehearsal is a self-fulfilling prophecy. If you put your head on the pillow at night and ask yourself, "How did my day go?" are you being proactive? No! The proactive route is to ask yourself "How do I want my day to go?" before it even begins. You can decide right then and there that you will have a 10 day.

Deciding to have a 10 involves Rox-Talk. Allowing yourself to keep that 10 all day long, no matter what it might bring, is also dictated by your Rox-Talk, not your circumstances.

Party Time

Let me give you an example of how Rox-Talk dictates thinking and actions. Let's pretend that one day, I call up a friend to invite him to a party I'm throwing at my house. I'm going to have a helicopter pick him up and fly him there—all expenses paid by me—and when he lands, he'll be picked up by Tina Fey and Chris Rock.

This is going to be a fantastic evening. But what if he considers himself shy? As he's on that helicopter nearing my party, what do you think his Rox-Talk is? "Will I know anyone there? What am I going to say to people? I can't talk to Chris Rock or Tina Fey. What would I say? I hope nobody talks to me at the party, either. I don't need *that*."

What is this Rox-Talk doing? It's dropping ROX the size of boulders in his negative bucket, and these ROX, in turn, are reinforcing his self-image. What self-image does this shy person have? How does he picture himself acting at a party? Shy. And how does this shy person behave at an event like this? He stands in a corner. What else? He disappears, or tries to. He's off to the kitchen; he's taking a walk around the yard.

Suppose this shy person walks around a corner and runs into Tina. She grabs my friend's hand, shakes it, and says, "Wow, I'm glad you're here! What's your name?"

What does the shy person do? He doesn't remember his name! He's too nervous. He's too shy. He knew his name when he arrived at the party. He's known his name for years. So what happens at that particular moment? Since his self-image dictates performance, his actions must follow. This is what's called his "performance reality."

What happens next? Tina laughs off the episode, she leaves, and the shy person stands there saying to himself, "I'm an idiot! I can't believe that happened. I never should have come to this party." His Rox-Talk is reinforcing his old beliefs. Most people would rather be right than successful. His Rox-Talk lowers his self-image even further, and his negative cycle continues.

It's a repeating pattern: **Our Rox-Talk** reinforces our **Self-Image**. Our **Performance Reality** (behavior) follows. This performance creates more **Rox-Talk**.

As you are placed into a situation—any situation—you are immediately making judgments about that situation based on your self-image. In your mind, you are deciding one of the following:

"That's not like me."

"That is like me."

Here's how this works: if Tina says to my shy friend, "I'm glad you're here. I've heard many good things about you," the shy person affirms to himself, "That's not like me." If Tina says, "I see that you're a little uncomfortable at this party. Is there anything I can do?" the shy person responds by affirming to himself, "That's like me." Rox-Talk continues to reinforce the existing self-image or, if you choose to change, Rox-Talk will create a new self-image. But it's your currently dominant self-image that will determine your actions/behaviors or your "performance reality." Remember the power of "sanity," or the currently dominant self-image. *We are programmed to look for information that will substantiate our beliefs or, in other words, make us right.*

> Once we decide how to act,
> our performance (behavior) follows.

How do you break this pattern? *By visualizing how you want to be and Rox-Talking that, rather than Rox-Talking how you've always been.* When you create new vision statements, you begin the process of Registering One Xperience neurologically. You begin the ROX-dropping process, which creates a new self-image that then changes your behavior. You can do this at home before you leave, or just before you step out of that helicopter. This is what I mean by "fixing your bike while you're riding it" or "living in the G.A.P." Living in the G.A.P. is where we truly maximize life's special moments. It is here where we take control and "changing our mind" begins. Creating a new perspective not only changes our mind, it changes our lives.

What Needs to Change?

Let's explore this further. I'd like to tell you now about a time when my self-esteem and my Rox-Talk were not at the level where they should've been. It was the early '80s, and I was on an airplane from Seattle to Washington, D.C. I had fortunately been upgraded to first class. The seat next to me was empty. Just as the doors were about to close, my seatmate arrived—Dr. Henry Kissinger, one of the most respected men in the world at that time.

I was blown away. I'd just finished reading *All the President's Men* and was well aware of how important Kissinger was. As I sat there, my Rox-Talk was going crazy. "That's Kissinger! This guy is brilliant! He got down on his knees to pray with Nixon!" But my Rox-Talk was also being influenced by my self-image at the time. "Too bad I'm not more interesting and more important. What the heck could *I* say to *Henry Kissinger?*" Needless to say, my Rox-Talk and my negative self-image were affecting my performance. I was glued to my seat, not saying a word.

The flight takes off. Mine was the window seat, and he was on the aisle. Kissinger's security was sitting immediately behind us. I discreetly stole glances at him. Kissinger was reading Gore Vidal's book about Lincoln, which was big at the time. In addition to the book, he had five or six newspapers from throughout the world jammed into the seat pocket in front of him, and a few other books at his side. I sat there feeling like I'd flunked the fourth grade! Was I comparing myself to Henry Kissinger? Absolutely! What would *he* possibly have to say to *me?* Comparisons are definitely the wrong road to take.

It was a long flight, six hours or so. Throughout the flight, I thought, "Larry, talk to him! That's Henry Kissinger! You might never have this opportunity again!" My self-image wouldn't let me say a word because it believed I had nothing of value to say.

We did speak once, briefly, during the flight. About halfway through the trip, I needed to use the restroom, so I leaned over to him and said, "Excuse me." He was very polite and said, "Sure." On the way to the restroom, I thought, "My gosh! Henry Kissinger talked to me! We're practically best friends now. When I get back to my seat, I'll call him Hank!" I didn't, of course; when I returned to my seat, I remained silent. My Rox-Talk was influencing my self-image, which was influencing my performance. I had my mind made up about what Dr. Kissinger thought of me, and didn't need to find out.

At last, the plane landed. As we taxied to the gate, the plane suddenly stopped. I peered out the window. A long limousine flanked with ten or twelve police cars idled on the tarmac. I don't know why I said it, but I turned to Dr. Kissinger and said, "Oh, I see they're waiting for me."

"Ho, ho, ho! That was a good one!"

I began to emerge from my shell. "Are you Dr. Henry Kissinger?"

"Yes, what's your name?"

"Larry Olsen."

Kissinger said, "Larry, I've been fascinated about you, but you don't talk much! Tell me about yourself!"

I said to myself, "You blew it, Larry, you idiot! You had six hours with this guy, and *now* you're talking to him!"

All I could manage to say was, "I must tell you this, I just finished *All the President's Men*."

"Where are you from?"

"Well, I'm from—I'm, uh … "

"We left Seattle. Maybe you're from Seattle?"

Why was I being such a loser that I couldn't even remember where I lived? According to my self-image, I wasn't on a level playing field with Henry Kissinger. I had no business even *talking* to him. The next thing I knew, he was out of his seat and off the plane. The limo pulled away, the police cars screamed off, and we continued to the terminal. He was gone. It's many years later now, and I haven't run into Hank again, but if I did, now I'd have some questions for him.

Our actions all get back to our self-image, don't they? And what affects our self-image? Our Rox-Talk. How can we change our Rox-Talk? Through vision statements, or by living in the G.A.P.—asking the question "How do I want it to be?" When we do that, we're using our "remotes" to change the channel. If you want to correct your performance—your behavior—what do you need to work on? Your thoughts! And how do you influence your thinking? Vision statements, and your "remote," or G.A.P. of opportunity.

What needs to change? Your Rox-Talk, because then your behavior will follow.

When do you need to be ready? Right now!

When do you need to feel how gifted and incredible you are? Right now!

Avoiding the Trap of Comparisons

The positive vision statements you create will help you avoid the trap of comparing yourself to others. That's what I was doing on that flight with Henry Kissinger. I was comparing my life to his. It's a very unfair thing to do to yourself or someone else. Of course, we've all been conditioned to compare ourselves to one another, and our culture focuses on what we do wrong, rather than what we do right. When you got back a graded test in school, what was marked—the 99 questions you answered correctly, or the one you got wrong? Is that a good way to build self-esteem?

Unfortunately, coaches can be the worst at building esteem. Not all of them, of course, but many. It's almost a militaristic model. "We're going to break you down and then we're going to build you up!" Unfortunately, some kids never get beyond the breaking-down part.

I'll give you an example. This is a story told by a great teacher I worked with for several years, Lou Tice. The high-school football team Lou coached was in a critical playoff game. Lou's team was behind by a touchdown. It was the fourth quarter, and they were jammed back near their own end zone. They needed a big punt from their kicker to keep the other team from scoring again.

The kicker, a junior, was a great player. Before he ran out onto the field, Lou grabbed him and said, "Whatever you do, don't screw up!"

Do we follow directions, or words?

The kicker ran out onto the field, and the team ran the play. The ball was snapped back to the punter, and he kicked it off the side of his foot. It went 10 yards and out of bounds, putting the other team in great shape to score again.

The punter ran off the field. Lou grabbed him and said, "What on earth did you do? We're in the game of our life and what do you do? You kick the ball off the side of your foot. Now sit down and think about it!"

Based on what you've learned about the power of Rox-Talk and its influence on behavior, what Lou told the punter demoralized him. Later, the kicker got a similar opportunity, and immediately kicked the ball off the side of his foot again. Lou became livid, telling him that he hadn't paid attention to their last conversation and that he was disappointed in him. Then he benched him. Lou's the one who should've been benched, of course, because the kid was doing exactly what he was being coached to do.

The remedy for this is as simple as it is powerful: tell people what to do right. After that first punt, Lou should have told the kicker, "Stop that! You're too good a kicker for that!"

This happens at our workplaces all the time. The boss walks in and says, "Don't screw up." The parent says, "Your room is a mess." Is that motivating? Would anyone feel good about working for or living with that person?

When you make a mistake, as we all do, say to yourself, "The next time something like this happens, I will do x, y, and z." Don't dwell on the problem. Focus on finding a solution. Use your Rox-Talk to program the correct image in your mind.

The same thing is true about the kind of day you want to have. Every morning when you wake up, say to yourself, "Something wonderful is going to happen to me today."

The positive self-esteem created through vision statements can snowball throughout your entire life. If you believe in yourself, you'll believe in others. That's why I encourage you to start inside your own mind. There's so much opportunity available to you. Don't miss these opportunities because you're being critical of yourself. The more critical you are of yourself, the lower your self-esteem will be. The more respectful you are of yourself and the more you focus on what's right about you, the more you raise your own self-esteem. Your performance will follow.

The Negative Power of Sarcasm

Since we're on the topic of building one's self-esteem, I'd like to bring up another element that can create powerful *negative* thoughts—sarcasm. Sarcasm has no place in a high-performance organization or a high-performance personal life.

Some of you may be thinking, "Excuse me? Sarcasm? That's something minor, it's harmless. Besides, that's a way of life in our company. That's a way of life in our family!"

The power of sarcasm is this: What a person says may be a harmless attempt to be funny, but no one can know how the target of the sarcasm will take it. That's where its negative power comes from.

I was giving a seminar one time, and during an early part of the first day, one of the participants raised his hand and asked, "Larry, do you have any sunglasses?"

"What for?" I said.

He replied, "To block out the glare from your forehead!"

Everyone in the room laughed. I had just turned 50 at the time, and I was thinning a little on top. (I still am!) On the outside, I was laughing too, but on the inside, I thought, "Ouch, that hurt! What a jerk!"

Some people say, "I just make fun of myself, not others," but that's the worst thing you can do. Your subconscious doesn't possess a sense of humor. It doesn't know that you're kidding. Remember, the subconscious can't differentiate between an actual event and ones we only imagine. If we make fun of ourselves, a ROX gets dropped in our negative bucket. Kidding or not, that ROX is still there. When we make fun of someone else, we always hit our mark; unfortunately, we never know what type of damage it has inflicted on the victim's self-esteem.

I've had people take exception to this suggestion. "Well, if I can't be sarcastic, what can I do?" *Avoid it!* True sarcasm's goal is to identify and amplify a weakness through humor. This should never be confused with having fun. When humor is at someone else's expense, negative ROX are being dropped. If you are truly serious about accomplishing more in the next year than you have in the last five, as well as bringing out the best in yourself and others, then I challenge you to take this pledge:

> *Beginning today, I will not allow any put-downs or hostility towards others or me. I will make no cynical statements, no snide*

remarks, no sarcasm, no cuts—not even for fun. I now know that the subconscious, which stores my self-image, cannot take a joke. It's like a robot that accepts what I say to myself, or what others say to me. If I slip and put someone else down, I affirm this statement: "That behavior is not like me. I constantly find ways to build myself and others up. The next time I will…" Go on to affirm what you will do when the next opportunity presents itself.

What about when people make fun of us? We can't stop that, but we can control our own behavior. The corporate world is the worst when it comes to sarcasm, because leaders are often the most sarcastic people. We can't control what others do or say, but I suggest this: stop doing it to yourself. No more, "That was stupid." You're brilliant! You're excellent. It doesn't get any better than you. Everything you do is marvelous. When you do make an occasional error, simply acknowledge it and attempt not to do or think the same thing again. Use this powerful mind shifter: "The next time I will…"

Living to Be 115

I'd like to spend a few moments on another topic that I think will help you break through to a life that ROX!

Pretend that you're standing in the middle of a normal-sized room. On the wall to your left, visualize your birth date, in big red letters. On the wall to your right, imagine that wall as your death—but don't assign a date to it. (Obviously, none of us know when we're going to die, and it's not a good idea to predict it.) Connecting the two walls is a piece of rope. This tightrope is your *lifeline*, your life as a series of days and weeks and years.

Next, think about tying a bright red ribbon on your lifeline that corresponds to where you are in your stage of life. If you're 20, your ribbon would be about a quarter of the way away from the left wall. If you're 90, your ribbon would be fairly close to the right wall. Put your ribbon wherever you want on your lifeline.

I'm not just an optimist. I'm also very analytical and scientific. Genetically, we are programmed to live as long as 140, but I also know that our culture plays a role in how long we live. To people in Nepal, living to 100 is common. Most people in the U.S. stress themselves into an early death.

But the L.I.F.E. lessons can help you extend your life. I certainly plan to live past the age of 115. I can see it myself: it'll be the year 2063, and when the "Today Show" runs through its 100+ birthday list, you'll hear "And happy birthday to Larry Olsen, who just turned 115!" You'll say to yourself, "I'll be darned, he looks fantastic! Wait a minute, I know him!"

Okay, where is your ribbon? Where on your lifeline is that ribbon attached? Stand under your ribbon, and face the wall with your birth date written on it. As you look at your past, see every single step that you've ever taken, every moment that you've experienced to get to this point in your life, as set in concrete. The concrete is 10 feet thick and dry as dust; it will never be changed. No matter what has happened to you up to this point in your life, get over it! Nothing in your past can be undone. There is no rewind button on life!

Next, turn your back on your birth date—your past—and face your future. Before you lies perfectly smooth, wet cement waiting for your next step. Your future is waiting for you to shape it.

The next time something happens to you, ignore everything you've learned in this book and look into your rear-view mirror and say, "Have I ever seen anything like this before? What's this leading me toward? Will this be good or bad?" You can make all the same decisions, and mistakes, that you've made before, and in a year all you will be able to say is that you're one year older. Growing a year older will be the major change in your life.

Or the next time something happens to you, say to yourself, "What step will I take to live my vision *right now?*"

Perhaps you're thinking, "Living to that age doesn't appeal to me. I'm already feeling the negative affects of aging." Get over it! How? Through a vision. You're not getting older, you're getting better. No matter what's happened in your past, you have the ability and the opportunity to live a life that ROX! *The physical and mental opportunities awaiting us are unlimited!* When are these opportunities available? These unlimited opportunities are available *right now,* and can be lived *right now* as you grow into your vision.

It's remarkable the power your thoughts can generate. With what you think, with what you believe, with what attitude you have, it's all just a matter of choice, and *the choice is yours.* Think about that. Congratulations. You have just become part of the one percent of the American population that knows how they think. Everyone else thinks about whatever is on their minds. They have no idea of the impact their thinking has on their behavior, because they are too busy thinking about the impact their behavior has on their lives. They believe that growth can only come with changing behavior.

Purpose: What's Yours?

You can't look to others for reinforcement or to model how you should think and act, because no one else is like you, and no one knows why you're here better than you.

What are you here for? You are here to make a difference. Everyone makes a difference, one way or the other. The question you have to ask yourself is this: "What kind of a difference do I want to make?"

The answer to that question will lead your way.

Who's on Their List?

Several years ago, I was asked to list the three most influential people in my life. After careful consideration I added my mom to my list. Why? Well, I decided to quit school in the first grade. I ended my academic career at the age of six. After a few severe humiliations, I'd had enough of the school and everyone in it. In the middle of the day, I trudged home, defeated. As I walked through the door, my mother, alarmed, wanted to know why I was crying and why I'd left school (reasonable questions, of course).

When I finally stopped crying, I told her what had happened. At that time in my life, I was covered with freckles, and my classmates had been making fun of them. I explained to her that I'd simply had enough, and that I wouldn't be going back. After my mom heard my story, she started to laugh. Somehow, I knew she wasn't laughing at me, but the situation.

She dried my tears, took me in her arms, and told me she had a secret to share with me. She whispered in my ear, "Larry, God gives freckles to the gifted ones. The reason your classmates are laughing at you is that it's their way of hiding their hurt, because they know they weren't as fortunate as you. Remember, those who don't know any better will always make fun of what they don't have or understand." That's all I'd needed to hear. With a smile on my face and a powerful secret in my mind, I returned to school.

Of course, my mom made that up. But the right words said at the right time by the right person can make all the difference in the world. That's why she made my list. If you make the same list of all the people who made the most positive difference in your life, they'd probably all have the same thing in common. They saw more in you than you did and brought out the best in you.

One day, people you know might be asked to make a list like that. Ask yourself, "Am I going to be on that list?" If the answer is "yes" keep being the best for the world, if the answer is no than ask yourself what you need to be doing that you're not doing now to get on the list.

Into the Future...Right Now

We've come a long way. I hope by now you have a better understanding of how your mind works and that you're confident you can positively affect your own thinking. This is why the Lessons in the Fundamentals of Excellence are so powerful and so exciting: You don't have to rely on anyone except yourself. You can't control what others say or do or think, but you can control your own thoughts.

We receive and become what we think about. Henry Ford once said, "Whether we think we can or think we can't, we're right." Your spouse or significant other, your kids, your friends, and your co-workers are in for a huge treat as you become the kind of person you were intended to be—an excellent one. Change yourself and others around you will change. Your L.I.F.E. is waiting. The choice is yours: What do you want to do with your life, and what do you want to become?

As we finish Lesson 8, I'd like to leave you with a final image. It's the theme song of life: "Row, Row Your Boat." Look at the song's lyrics carefully.

Row, row, row: The song says to row. It doesn't say, "Put a super-charged turbo engine on it, and go as fast as you can!" Move forward with determination and dedication, but enjoy yourself along the way, too. Don't turn life into a race. The speed of rowing is just right to enjoy life's precious moments without dwelling too long on any of them.

Your boat: Your boat, not someone else's. This doesn't mean that we can't row together, but we each have our own boats. There's never been another boat like yours, or mine, in the history of man. (You stay out of my boat and I'll stay out of yours.)

Gently down the stream: How should you row? Upstream, fighting all the way? Resisting new ideas? No, you should row gently down the stream that flows with life. It's a perfect rhythm to live by.

Merrily, merrily, merrily: Your attitude while rowing should be a positive one... *merrily, merrily, merrily...*because ...

Life is but a dream! Why should you be having the time of your life *right now? Because life is but a dream!* It's your life, so what's your dream? You now have the awareness and the tools, so...

Create your vision and live every moment you are given as if it is the most important one of your life, because it is.

Remember "Row, Row, Row Your Boat." I tweaked Thoreau a bit; *as you row confidently in the direction of your dreams and endeavor to live the life you have imagined, you will meet with success unexpected in common hours.*

A Final Note

We've come a long way to get here. We've all had our trials and tribulations, but no matter what the circumstances are, we can choose to find the magnificence in each moment. I'm confident that by now you've seen and experienced how powerful the Lessons In the Fundamentals of Excellence can be. Imagine the possibilities once you put them into action.

Now I'd like to end this section of the book by restating many of the key points needed for you to Get a Vision and Live it!

- *The vision comes first, and then you will witness the evidence necessary to succeed.*

- *Decide what you want, and the "how" will come naturally.*

- *When you have a vision—and believe in it—nothing can stop you.*

- *You deserve to have the time of your life right now.*

- *Live the vision every single day. If you're living the vision, your attitude and behavior will follow.*

- *The only way you can change is by changing your perspective and taking action right now.*

- *The only reason you're not succeeding right now is that your vision of what you want isn't strong enough.*

- *Your self-image, your Roxometer, lies within you.*

- *When you look forward, endorphins are released in the brain—an incredible feeling.*

- *Everything you have right now in your life is what you feel that you deserve.*

- *If perfection is your vision, you're in trouble. Do not attempt to achieve perfection; strive for excellence instead. Excellence is simply letting your God-given talents and joy out for yourself and others to experience.*

When you face the future, I hope you see nothing but fresh, wet, smooth concrete ahead. It's there, waiting for you to make a mark on this world in your life and in the lives of others. Make your next choice *the choice of vision!*

Lesson 8
Reflection Questions

How can the Rox-Talk rehearsal ultimately change your behavior?

What are ways to build yourself up? Why is this so essential in living an inspired life?

What specifically do you need to do to bring out the best in yourself?

In your spouse or significant other?

In your children?

In your co-workers and friends?

List the areas you need to work on to honestly say that you're having the time of your life *right now*:

I can take away the following insight from this lesson ...

I intend to use it first in the areas of ...

Because ...

List the behaviors you would like to change or visions you would like to accomplish:

APPLYING THE L.I.F.E.
LESSONS

Making Time for Your L.I.F.E.

"Live your life as if you've already arrived; after all, when you really think about it, you have." — Larry Olsen

In this section, I'd like to give you specific suggestions and ideas to help you apply the Lessons In the Fundamentals of Excellence in your life. *Taking action* on a daily basis is critical to success. No matter how well you understand how you think and how you can influence and affect your life and the lives of others. Little, if anything, will happen unless you actively apply what you've learned.

Here are suggestions to help you find—I like to say "make"—time to begin creating your vision statements and reviewing them on a daily basis.

1. Carve out time to create your vision statements.

As you realize by now, creating your vision statements will require time and energy on your part. You'll want to take time to explore areas of your life that you want to change, and put on paper precisely what it is that you want to do or become. Time, however, is something most of us don't have enough of.

Here are some specific ways to "make" some time during your day to create vision statements:

- Use fifteen minutes of your lunch hour

- Get up thirty minutes earlier than normal

- Watch one less TV show each evening

- Use your phone, and record thoughts and observations while driving

- Set aside at least thirty minutes on a particular evening each week

- Set aside at least thirty minutes at a certain point in each weekend, such as first thing Saturday morning or late Sunday afternoon

Whenever you think about what you don't want, or what you wish would change, what better opportunity to write or record a vision statement by simply asking, "How would I describe myself when it's the way I want it to be?"

What other ways or times in your life can you "make time" to work on your vision statements? The opportunities are there, if you look for them.

2. Review your vision statements daily.

I suggest that you spend a minimum of 10 minutes a day reviewing your vision statements. You should break this up into two separate times: five minutes in the morning after you've awakened, and five more minutes at night, right before you fall asleep. That may not seem like a huge time commitment, but you'd be surprised how many people come back to me and say, "Ten minutes! Are you crazy? Do you know how busy I am?"

This review process is essential, because you receive tremendous benefits by programming your vision statements into your subconscious. If you continue to have difficulty carving out time to review your vision statements, write a vision statement about it, like:

> I feel elated, energized, and vibrant because of the quick and positive results I receive from reading and visualizing my vision statements daily.

Think of reviewing your vision statements as going to your own movies. What do you see? How do you feel? What are you doing that you are proud of? Let your imagination loose. When you think about it, just skipping one two hour movie, that's in no danger of changing your life, is 12 days of visioning.

Why read them in the morning and at night? Because those are the times that people are most susceptible to suggestion. You can read them any time you want, of course, but these are the most productive times to do so.

Your mind is programming your RAS while you're reading your vision statements, and you're reminding yourself of how you want to be—*right now*. Not next week, and not "as soon as…" *Right now.*

Imagine how your life would transform if the first thing you did each morning was read this vision statement:

> I feel valued, loved, and incredible because
> I greet my family with a smile and give them each a hug.

or

> I look for and see in each one of them what
> I love most about them and remind them of how incredible they are.

What great vision statements, right? It's simple, too, but even the simplest vision statements can be challenging. For those of us who have children, mornings can be especially stressful. There are breakfasts to make, last-minute homework assignments to finish, lunches to prepare, and so on. This vision statement will help you even in the craziest of times. Choose to find ways to be the best for others.

3. Do what works for you.

My suggestions here are just that—suggestions. Feel free to modify when you create and review your vision statements *based on your own particular needs and schedule*.

For example, I know some people who review their career- and work-related vision statements before they begin their workday and review family-related vision statements before they return home at night. Doing so helps them refocus and make the transition from work to home more smoothly.

You can also verbally record your vision statements and play them back at various times, such as in the car. This method is an excellent way to "find time" to review your vision statements instead of listening to news or music on the radio on your way to and from work.

4. Start small and build up over time.

Another question I frequently receive is this: how many vision statements should I have? I recommend that you begin small. Create between six and 12 vision statements and review them for several weeks. As you get more comfortable with this routine, create more.

I currently read 12 vision statements every morning and every night. (I've read as many as 50—the point is, there is no magic number.) Doing it takes me about five minutes each morning and five minutes each night. I could spend as little 10 seconds with each one, but I've found that the more time I spend envisioning each statement, the faster the change takes place. I strongly urge you to find those 10 minutes. When your subconscious receives your vision statement, it believes as fact. You are programming yourself to have what you want and achieve the things you want to achieve.

It's important to remember to first set visions in all areas of your life before writing more than one in each area. The 30 plus that I currently read cover eight general areas. This assures balance in your life.

5. You can't just go through the motions—you must first believe.

How much conviction should you put behind your vision statements? Is complete conviction essential? Yes. You must first believe, and then you will see. Get psyched up about your visions and put some excitement behind them. Ask yourself: "What will my life be like when I achieve this? Would there be any value to my life if this vision became reality?" If you answer, "My life would be a little better," tear it up. It's not doing what it should do—get you incredibly excited. You only want vision statements that make you say, "That would be fantastic!"

Believing you'll achieve your vision statements requires faith. You're up against powerful forces—your current reality and your past experiences, but those forces are minimal compared to the power of your own mind and vision. You've had an awful lot of ROX thrown in your buckets.

By the way, I'm not only talking about faith in a religious sense. Sometimes when the word faith makes people uncomfortable—particularly in corporate America. When I talk about faith, I'm talking about a mental attitude, one so utterly entrenched that any contradiction is unthinkable and impossible. In other words, if you have faith, you believe something is a done deal. You believe the change cannot not happen.

Again, this all gets back you. *You* must first believe—not your spouse, not your kids, not your boss, and not your teammates. Only you. If you want recognition, go outside yourself. If you want power—power over your limiting beliefs—go inside yourself.

What If I Fail?

Let's talk more about faith in our visions, because it's essential to your growth and success. Metaphorically, we're all from Missouri—"the show-me state." We want to see proof. We're paying attention to the evidence, but forgetting the vision.

This "show-me" attitude is particularly prevalent when we fail. Failure is not a reflection on you or your abilities; it simply means that your vision isn't strong enough yet, and what you tried didn't work. Failure doesn't mean you don't work, or that you're never going to be able to achieve your vision. You simply made the wrong turn. When we know the destination (vision) we recognize that it's frustrating when we make the wrong turn. It may have taken us hours, weeks or years off of course, but it doesn't mean we can't find our way. We just need to find another way. If you want the vision bad enough, you'll find another way.

When you do fail, you must strengthen your vision. (I don't even like the word "failure," because of the negative connotations it has and how it makes me feel.) I consider any of my accomplishments—whether or not they succeed—to be "evidence." If the evidence suggests that I'm on the right track to vision, I continue my efforts in that direction. If the evidence shows that I'm on the wrong track, I use that feedback as positive information to get me on the right track. Either way, I don't lose, and as long as my vision is strong enough and important enough, nothing can stop me but myself.

You must still believe, even when you experience failures. Let me tell you about W. Clement Stone. He became a self-made millionaire in the 1930s, when a million dollars meant quite a bit more than it does now. Stone referred to himself as an "inverse paranoid." He believed the universe was conspiring to do him good. Isn't that a great belief? Think what our lives would be like if each of us affirmed that idea every day.

Stone had a phrase he referred to over and over again: "Something wonderful is going to happen to me today." Imagine what Stone's RAS was open to. Imagine what he was on the lookout for every day—good things. When things went well, his Rox-Talk would say, "That's just what I expected."

Whenever something went wrong—and something almost always did—Stone would ask, "What is this gift teaching me today?" What a great question! Instead of a problem, Stone saw a potential gift, a way to learn. When you approach problems with this attitude, you will see gifts. You will learn important lessons. There's no other option.

You also won't be held hostage by the negative emotions around you. Do you want an invisible shield to protect you from challenges and problems? Do you want to counter the negative things in your life *right now?* Don't do it with fists. Use words instead. Say to yourself, "That's not me. I know who I am. I am calm and relaxed. I easily handle one thing at a time, and I do first things first." Can you handle more than one thing at a time and still be effective?

A Final Note

The best intentions and the best knowledge are useless unless they are applied. You now have an incredible understanding and foundation regarding your thinking and your ability to do or become what you want, but knowledge alone isn't enough. You must take action on a daily basis. You know what you know. Until you change your knowledge, you won't change your life.

In addition to taking daily action on your vision statements, you must expect good things to happen to you. Visualize in your mind what you want to achieve or become, and these visions will become reality.

> People who hope to change create wishes;
> people who know how to change realize their visions.

A Note to
Parents and Spouses

*" The secret is not in how you raise them,
but in how you praise them."*
—Larry Olsen

B y now, you realize how powerful the L.I.F.E. lessons can be. Nowhere is there greater opportunity for fulfillment and a sense of peace than when interacting with your children. The quality of our relationships determines the quality of our lives. The same applies to your spouse or significant other. In no other part of your life is the potential to grow and become fulfilled more important than in the relationship with your partner.

Let's look at some specific ways you can make a huge positive impact on the lives of your family and friends.

Learn to Listen

We all want someone to care about us. This is particularly true with children. One way to show others you care is to listen to them. If you listen to someone, particularly a child, you become their best friend. Remember, the moment I make you number one and put myself second, I become number one in your mind. You will always be treated by others the way you treat them.

Let me give you an example of what can happen when you listen to a child. One day when she was six, my daughter Courtney wanted to show me a picture she was proud of. But there was a problem: I was reading a very important article in the newspaper.

Courtney said, "Dad, look!"

"Just a minute, honey."

Courtney persisted. "Dad, look!"

"Just a minute, honey."

"Dad, look!"

"Just a minute, honey."

Was anybody winning here? Was I reading the article? No. Were Courtney's needs being met? No. Was I listening to her? No! We do this all the time with people we love.

The wonderful thing, though, is that you always get another shot to jump into the G.A.P. I finally put the paper down, and when Courtney asked me to look at her picture, I said, "What do you want to show me?"

"Look at this picture I drew."

"Wow! What a beautiful picture, honey!"

"Thanks!"

I could've ended the conversation right there, of course, but I didn't. I seized the opportunity. "What are you most proud of in this picture?"

She said, "Do you see what's next to the little girl?"

Her insistence and enthusiasm were infectious. I looked more closely at the picture and said, "I hadn't noticed that. What is it?"

"You don't know what it is?"

I was feeling pressure, so I hedged a bit. "I want you to tell me, sweetie."

Courtney said, "It's a turtle, Dad."

"Wow! How come it's in the picture?"

"That's why I wanted you to watch it, Dad. It's a magic turtle."

"Yeah? What kind of magic can it do?"

"It can make your wishes come true."

"Really? Are you wishing for something?"

"Dad, my first wish was that you would look at my picture."

190

I was stunned, but I recovered quickly. "Did you get your wish, honey?" I asked.

"I did, Dad! Thanks, and you can too."

Wow!

I consider myself a very loving father, but it's difficult sometimes to be "there" all the time with your family, right? I've got a career to build. I've got places to go and people to meet. I've got important things to do. Be careful of this sentiment: "Someday, my children will be proud of me." You want your children to be proud of you *right now*.

No matter how busy you are, when you have the opportunity to listen to your children, do it. Drop everything. Throw the remote on the ground. Tell your children, "Talk to me! Tell me what it is you did today. I want to know what you are proud of." Listen, and watch what happens as a result!

Always be certain you're really listening. People—and especially children— almost always know if you're saying one thing and doing another. Authenticity is the key; put belief behind your words. Your words, body language, and tone of voice must all match. Approach it with love rather than impatience.

Prompt Your Children

Your children aren't always going to want to communicate. It will often be up to you to initiate these interactions. They don't have to be "serious" talks, either. Little opportunities can make big differences in your life.

Here's how I prompt my children to open up. When your children talk to you about something they've accomplished, ask them, "Why are you so proud of this?"

Often, you'll get an answer like, "Can't you tell, Dad?"

"I want to hear it from you. Why are you so proud of this?"

Listen to what your child has to say. As you do, you will learn volumes about who they really are. When you realize that your next question comes from the last thing they share with you, you'll spend more time listening instead of thinking about what you plan to say next. Listening unconditionally is truly the greatest gift you can give to another person.

Making a Difference That Lasts a Lifetime

Here's another opportunity to learn how your kids are thinking and what's important in their lives. It's also a wonderful exercise to raise self-esteem and to develop positive attitudes in your children and yourself. Right before they fall asleep at night, ask them, "What were you most proud of today?" When they tell you, then ask, "Why?" Each time they respond, continue asking why until they can't answer any longer. After that, ask, "What are you looking forward to tomorrow?" Again, find out why.

You can do the same thing with your spouse or even a close friend.

"What are you most proud of today?"

"Why?"

"What are you looking forward to tomorrow?"

"Why?"

It doesn't matter how many children you have or how old they are. It's a great exercise for grandparents too. Ask these questions, and you will receive incredible insights into your children's thinking. Ask, and it shall be given to you.

I started this with my son Don one night. "What were you most proud of today?" I asked him.

At the time, Don was in the fourth grade. It's an age when kids question everything, particularly their parents. He said, "Why do you want to know?"

I hadn't asked too often before, had I? I replied, "Because I'm interested, Don."

He said, "Dad, I am most proud of recess."

I was very tempted to fall into the parent trap of hearing an answer and relating it to myself: "Now I know what he's talking about—I used to enjoy recess myself." When we do, we shut ourselves off to what our kids are really trying to tell us. Don't go there. Keep asking, probing below the surface. Rediscover your children instead of attempting to identify with them by sharing a similar experience you once had. Always block out your "I had it once" with their "I'm having it now," if you really want to listen.

"Why are you proud of recess?" I asked.

He said, "Because I kicked the ball through the goal, Dad!" He was really into soccer back then.

"How did scoring that goal make you feel, Don?"

"It made me feel wonderful!"

"How does wonderful make you feel?"

He thought for a moment. (Remember what is happening neurologically. He is dropping ROX in his soccer Roxometer. The more the emotion, the faster the change. I wanted him to think about what he meant and use feeling words to make an even stronger impact on his subconscious picture of his soccer experience.) "Dad, wonderful feels like tingles all over my body."

"Is that a good thing?"

"It's amazing."

I said, "Cool!" But I didn't stop there. Don was really sleepy, but I asked, "And what are you looking forward to tomorrow?"

"Recess!"

Like any other parent, I wished he'd said "science" or maybe "English." It would've been cool if he'd said, "I can't wait for math, Dad, because I'm going to solve an equation that's going to provide inexpensive energy for the whole world!" But I was listening to my son, not judging him. "Why are you looking forward to recess?" I asked.

"I get to play soccer again."

"I see. And why are you looking forward to playing soccer again?

"I've been thinking about how good I felt when I kicked the ball, Dad, but I also remember how bad Matt felt when I kicked it. Tomorrow, Dad, I'm looking forward to passing the ball to Matt, so he can kick it."

"How is that going to make you feel?"

"Matt is my best friend, and seeing him happy is a great feeling for me too."

"Great," I said. "Good night, Don."

I do this often when I'm putting my children to bed. The opportunity to learn from them and about them is amazing. We have to ask. We have to listen. We can't let our lives get in the way of what we're hearing. We need to be more like strangers asking for directions. *Remember, we're not held back by what we know, but by thinking that we know.*

I asked Don this question every night for two weeks. Then one afternoon, I picked Don up after school. At the school, pick-up time was crazy—cars everywhere, inching along, to pick up the kids. As I drove along the back side of the school, I saw Don walking toward the edge of the playground. I timed it perfectly, so I'd arrive right in front of the school just as Don reached the pick-up area. But when I drove up, Don wasn't there. I had to move quickly, because there were other parents waiting in line to pick up their kids.

Finally, I saw Don. He was still on the playground with another kid. I started to get uptight. I knew that I couldn't sit there and wait, because the parents behind me would get upset. I had things to do, too; my time was valuable. I began to white-knuckle the steering wheel, and Don was still messing around with some kid. The woman behind me honked her horn. I gave her a little wave, but in my head, I was yelling, "Don, would you hurry up? You know better than this!"

Now the teachers began to glare at me because they knew I knew better, but I'd be darned if I was going to give up. To give up meant driving out of line, around the block again, and through two stoplights. And if that wasn't enough, the high school across the street was going to be letting out all the students as well—soon the whole area would be a real nightmare. That'd be another fifteen minutes out of my life, right?

I moved slowly ahead about two feet, to give the illusion that I was moving. It didn't work. The parents behind me started honking more. Then, I saw Don running, but not to the car. He was running back into the building! I was furious. Don knew better that this.

Don finally finished fooling around with the other kid and came running across the playground. Just before he jumped in the car, I prepared to read him the riot act, telling him how rude he'd been and what a frustrating position he had left me in. But I stopped. I put into practice what you've been reading about. I created the GAP. In my mind, I said, "Stop, Larry! You're better than this. You are calm and patient."

I relaxed. Don got in the car and said, "Dad, I am so sorry I kept you waiting in line! That was Cameron. He's physically handicapped, and I was helping him with his backpack because I knew tonight you were going to ask me what I was most proud of today."

Wow. How close was I to missing that? If I had yelled at Don, he never would have told me that he was helping Cameron. He would have sunk down in the seat and shut his mouth, and we would have driven home in angry silence.

The opportunities are all around us if only we'd take the time to experience them.

What happened to Don? By asking him every night what he was looking forward to the next day, his RAS was open and looking for the opportunities that he could be proud of. What a great habit to develop! Everybody wants their children to have high self-esteem. Asking the right questions and listening can do wonders to promote this.

Some of you might be thinking, "Oh, no—my children are grown! They've already left the house!" If this is the case, you have a huge opportunity: *You get to rediscover your own children.* Considering all the years you had with them, it

194

may be tempting to assume that you "know them." But they are not the children you once knew. They have their own lives and their own ways of thinking. You can rediscover them by listening to them and asking questions based on what you hear them say, rather than what you've come to know about them.

To do it, you'd say something like this: "Hi, Gretchen" [my oldest, extremely bright, and loving daughter]. "How'd your day go?…What did that make you feel like? …What do you plan on doing about it?…Is that something that you are looking forward to?…I'll call you again soon so you can let me know how it went."

Instead of: "Hi, Gretchen. Are you still disappointed in your job? How many resumes have you written? You know how you are, honey. Procrastination never got anything in the mail. Blah, blah, blah, blah, blah."

That's not letting go of how I know her. We're not in any danger of rediscovering our children or spouses if we keep hanging on to what we think we already know about them. Gretchen would certainly not look forward to phone calls like that.

You can also begin raising your own self-esteem by asking yourself these same questions just before you fall asleep. Even I have days when the only thing I can come up with is, "I got dressed all by myself today. I didn't need any help!" (We all have those kinds of days, don't we?) But finding something that I'm proud of doesn't allow me to dwell on those things I'm not.

When you start asking yourself these questions, over time you'll build up your self-esteem and confidence. When you ask yourself, "What am I looking forward to tomorrow?" you'll also improve your sleep beyond your wildest imagination. Too many of us try to strategize and to figure everything out, or replay the past. Either process leads to poor sleep. Sometimes, even after sleeping eight hours, you're still exhausted, because you've been battling all night. You have an incredible brain than can resolve any issue—as long as you program it in advance to open you up to the resolution of your challenge. Have confidence that it will, so you can sleep in the meantime and get that "ah-ha" the next day.

Building Self-Esteem in Children

Most of what we've discussed in this chapter on children has been focused on building relationships, but building a child's self-esteem is just as important.

Children are amazing. If you discover life along with them, you'll find yourself discovering how to truly live in the now. If you attempt to grow them into what *you* want them to be, all you'll ever know about them is what they think you want to hear. When we treat children with respect, confidence, and enthusiasm, we're building their self-esteem.

A C.E.O. of successful company was once asked what his favorite word was.

His answer was a little unexpected: "Yes." He uses it in his business as often as he possibly can. When someone on his staff asks him if they can do something, his answer is usually, "Yes."

What's the favorite word of most parents? "No," of course. Some defer the question: "Well, maybe…Let's think about it." There's also, "Go ask your mother," or "We'll let you know what we decide." The message they send their children with any of these forms of "no" is, *"Let me kill your spirit. Let me stomp on you for a little while, and then come back. Later, if you're still strong about it, maybe we'll take a look at it."* These messages lower self-esteem, clearly.

Why are we afraid to say "yes"? Perhaps because we fear they will walk all over us. I agree that young people need parameters, but is that what *all* our "no's" are about? Are they *all* in the name of safety? Or are they really more about control? Ironically, you have the most control when you give control up. That's a scary thought for some, but it's true. Self-reliance and accountability occur when children are given the opportunity to have some control over their own lives. Just look at your own childhood. What did you learn from it? If you could have been your own parent, would you have done anything differently? So why don't you do it now?

Remember Albert Bandura? To build your own self-esteem, Bandura found, you must look back at your life and see all the things you messed up and all the tragedies you experienced. Then, he recommends, rather than dwelling on these times, you must reflect on how you pulled yourself up and moved forward. That's where strength comes from. When most people would have given up and backed away, you came back.

This is never truer than with your children. If you have kids, you're going to make an occasional mistake. In fact, you're probably going to make many of them. You're going to say something or do something that you'll regret. You can't dwell on these occasional lapses; you must move on.

I don't want this next part to get too soft, so to speak, but there is no wrong that love can't overcome, and there is nothing that love eventually can't penetrate. When you look into someone's eyes and tell him or her with your heart and soul, "I know I haven't made all the right decisions in my life, but I just want you to know that I love you," nothing can break that down or make that go away.

It doesn't matter what you do as a parent. If your child knows that you love him or her unconditionally, you will have succeeded in life far beyond your wildest expectations. A wonderful psychology professor once gave me some excellent parenting advice: "Forget about all the stupid comments and mistakes you ever made. As long as your children know you love them unconditionally, you've succeeded as a parent." What could be simpler? The key is the "unconditional" part.

Learn from Your Children

A final point I'd like to make about children is that you should certainly teach them whenever possible, but you shouldn't miss the opportunities to learn from them, either.

Kids are amazing and very creative. Often, when you buy a child a toy, he or she ends up being far more interested in the box it came in than the toy. The toy is a toy; it's limited by what it's supposed to be and do. A box, on the other hand, can be *anything!* Your opportunities with your children, spouse, and friends are as endless as a child's imagination.

One day, Tori, my youngest daughter, came home from preschool in tears. I asked her what was bothering her, and she said, "I can't read." She hadn't learned how to read yet, but some of her classmates had.

I took her in my arms, looked her in the eyes, and said, "That's why you're in school, honey, to learn how to read. It's okay not to know yet. You can't know any more than what you have learned. When you learn, you will know."

She gave me a kiss, jumped out of my arms, and went off to play. The lesson she taught me was so powerful, that I somehow I felt lighter once I'd learned it. We can't be any better than the information we have now. To get better, we simply need to choose information that matches what we want. We need to stay in the school of life, ask when we don't know, and say "yes" to every opportunity. Remember, the word "no" keeps us from growing into the life we've never had and the word "yes" allows us to experience the life we're supposed to have.

Connecting with Your Spouse

Our relationships with significant others are also vitally important parts of our lives. Many of the same points I just covered about children also apply to relationships with spouses. One of the focuses is listening to your spouse. Listen up, and drop what you're doing. Throw the remote on the ground and say, "Talk to me! Tell me your story. Tell me about your day, about what got you excited. Talk to me." Just watch what happens as a result.

And just like with your children, when you do this, never, ever, ever, expect something in return! Listen unconditionally. Do something nice, with no ulterior motive, for the other person. *Manipulation is the greatest insult we can give to our fellow man.*

Let me tell you a story of mine, a time when this *didn't* happen. (I've made a lot of mistakes, as you now know, and I'll make more! But I don't dwell on those mistakes other than to learn from them; I use my vision statements to grow.) One evening, the children were staying overnight at friends' houses, without any input from my wife I planned an incredible evening. I really wanted to make the evening special, because I was looking forward to the last part of the evening, if you know what I mean.

I decided to do something nice for Diane. I got home early, before she got home, and immediately began cleaning the house. Believe me, this wasn't something I normally look forward to doing; but I had a vision and wanted to impress Diane. Once I finished cleaning the house, I began cooking. Once a few dishes were going, the kitchen began to smell wonderful.

But I didn't stop there. I got a portable fan, put it in the kitchen, and aimed it toward the rest of the house, so Diane would smell the food when she entered. I was really zooming—good smells, the house was clean, and everything was going as planned. And what was my plan? In my mind, I just knew that Diane was going to come home, see the house, and think, "Wow!" She'd smell the dinner I was cooking, and be so appreciative that she'd run into the kitchen to tell me how incredibly thoughtful I am. We would both enjoy a "10" evening. That was my vision for the night. It doesn't *sound* like manipulation, does it?

A little later, I heard the door open. As I heard Diane coming toward the kitchen, I got more and more pumped up, because I'd been working hard and was ready for my reward. (I don't know if this is a male thing or not, but it seems to me that whenever men do something, they expect to have an award handed to them as soon as possible.) Anyway, I could still hear Diane's footsteps, but instead of getting louder, the sound was drifting *away*. She was walking away from the kitchen.

My emotions began to drop. I thought to myself, "What's going on here? Diane is supposed to be coming *into* the kitchen, not going *away from it*." I began to cop a negative attitude. I begin to get upset—OOPS. "I did all this work. She should've spotted that I cleaned the house. She should've smelled that I'm cooking dinner!" I had even left flowers in the foyer!

I went into the living room. The house looked great. I could smell the flowers. I could smell the dinner. But Diane hadn't said a word. The more I thought about her silence, the more upset I became. I went back into the kitchen and what happened? My attitude translated into behavior, and I started slamming things around. I began banging pots and pans.

Remember our discussion about scotomas? One of the problems with scotomas is that we don't know that we have them. All of sudden, Diane entered the kitchen. She said, "Honey?"

"What?" I didn't even look up at her.

"What's wrong?"

You know the answer to that, right? Deny, deny, deny. "Nothing!" I said. "Nothing's wrong!"

But something was wrong. It was too late for her to rescue the evening, because she didn't fulfill *her* part of *my* plan. She didn't read her script. I'd put forth a significant effort for her, and she didn't do what I wanted her to do!

The entire time, I didn't even look at her because I was too upset. Finally, she said, "Wow, you cleaned the house, and the flowers are wonderful. And I see that you cooked, too."

"Yeah, I cooked." My eyes remained fixed on the countertop. They should have been looking at her. When Diane walked through the door, she'd seen that I had cleaned the house, noticed the flowers I'd bought, and smelled the dinner I was cooking. But instead of coming directly into the kitchen, she'd gone into the bedroom, slipped into something more comfortable, and put on my favorite perfume. *Then* she came into the kitchen.

I didn't see her, though. I didn't even smell her perfume. Why? Because I had created a huge scotoma for myself. There went my 10.

Don't try to control your spouse's behavior. You'll set yourself and your spouse up for failure, every time. Instead, set a vision for yourself, for your actions and behaviors, and let others do whatever they choose to do. Do it because you want to, not because you want something in return. Ulterior motives will get you nowhere. As long as I make you number one and put myself second, I'll always be number one in your eyes.

Setting visions for yourself is important in communicating with your partner, just as it is with your children. Don't make your mind up about a person or situation ahead of time, unless it's to see them as a gift you have the opportunity to open through questions driven by love. Once you ask the questions, really listen to the answers. Be enlightened by what's said or done, because you haven't heard it before. Make a connection. Remember that you're watching your partner's movie. It benefits not only the relationship, but both of you as individuals. *When we rediscover others, we rediscover ourselves.*

I challenge you to reconnect with your spouse. Don't figure out the "how" first, because, as you now know, the "how" is a by-product of the vision.

And don't put it off, either. Don't wait until "tomorrow," or "when the kids are out of the house." Do it *right now*. Take action *right now*.

A Final Note

In this section, we've talked mostly about the importance of building great relationships with your children and with your significant other, but this message also applies to all the people you are close to in your life—parents, siblings, cousins, and friends. Create visions that help you become the best *for* the relationship, rather than the best in the relationship. That is truly one of the most rewarding parts of life: helping others grow, helping others build their self-esteem, and helping others become who they want to become.

What we're talking about here is having a purpose in life aimed at helping others. Passion is the essence of life, and we get passion from purpose. If one of your purposes in life is to help others, I guarantee you that you will find more joy and passion than you've ever dreamed is possible.

Please remember one more thing: You cannot give other people your vision. That's up to them. But you can control your own visions, thoughts, and actions. As you think about the visions you're creating, always ask yourself: "What kind of difference am I making in the lives of others? Will I make their list of the three most influential people in their lives?

A Note to
Managers and Leaders

"When I asked why the leadership was so loved and respected, I learned that they always saw more in me than I did, and never let me let myself down."

– Larry Olsen

A lmost all of us are involved in the work world—working with others for a common end result—to some degree. Even if you're independently wealthy and volunteer at a nonprofit agency, you're still working with others to accomplish a common vision.

Because they work with others, managers and business leaders are in a position to influence—either positively or negatively—the lives of co-workers and the self-esteem and confidence of others beyond the workplace. How they treat their employees has a domino effect that can even effect the grades that those employees' children earn. It is a huge responsibility, a responsibility with potential ramifications larger than most people in the business world realize.

Vision Is the Key

The best leaders bring out the best in others. When I use the term "leaders," I mean that in the broadest sense possible. Even if no one reports to you, or if you do not technically "lead" anyone else, you are still a leader, because you are leading yourself. If you do so unselfishly, the model you create automatically brings about positive change in others. To me, everyone is a leader.

Unfortunately, most of corporate America relies on fear to motivate employees. "You'd better do it, or you'll get the ax." "You'd better say or think this, or you won't be part of the 'team.' This type of leadership is anything but inspiring, and it's no way to build self-esteem in others. Self-esteem and performance go hand-in-hand. Raise self-esteem, and you raise performance. Lower it, and, well, you know the rest.

Leaders do not bring out the best in someone by finding fault with him or her. The people under a leader who does this will not rally around that leader. In fact, the opposite will happen.

This all gets back to attitude, as this chart illustrates:

Leader's Attitude	How Others React
Arrogance	Develop low self-esteem.
Humility	Wanting to be around leader.
Telling, ordering	Doing enough to get the leader to shut up, and then stand around waiting for further instructions or trying to "look busy."
Listening	Exceeding expectations while becoming highly creative.

A leader should be an inspirational factor in the lives of others. Let's make this even simpler, because a leader's job is simple. Whether you are a parent, a teacher, a manager, or a business owner, as a leader, your job is to *create an environment where others can succeed.* The moment I make you number one and put myself in second place, I will always be number one in your mind.

If you set a vision and create an environment for others to grow and succeed, they will, but too often, leaders just give orders. They tell others what to do, "strongly suggesting" that certain things be done, certain actions be taken, and certain attitudes be held. It's all about manipulation. When leaders do this, employees accept it because they feel they have to, but they will only give back just enough to get the job done. They won't go any further than they have to.

Do you want to be a great leader? Are you interested in becoming one? Then act like one—*right now.* I'll share an interesting story with you that happened several years ago. I was on site at a client organization and was asked to do a one-on-one coaching session with a salesperson. About a half-hour into the session, the discussion turned to management. He admitted that he would have loved to have been a manager, but he believed that he was too old.

I asked, "Why do you think you could make a contribution to the organization?"

He replied that he had run his own company for years and spent years before that in several management positions. He felt that considering his experience, as well as the fair share of the wisdom he'd gained with age, his leadership would be extremely beneficial to his company.

I asked him why he wasn't pursuing his vision. He replied, "Do you know what the average age in this company is? 26. And I'm 50."

I said, "Let me see if I understand what you just said. You feel that you would bring value to the growth of this company, but because of your age, you are in no danger of making it into management. Is that the gist of your story?"

He nodded and said, "That's it."

I asked him another question. "Have you let anyone know that you want to get into management?"

"Why would I do that?" he replied. "Didn't you get the age thing, Larry?"

"No, I didn't get the age thing," I said. "What I got was the excuse thing." I then asked him if he wanted my feedback, and he said that was why he was talking to me in the first place.

I told him that the "age thing" was *his* thing, not the company's, unless he vocalized it. If he was interested in getting into management, he needed to take two very important steps: First, he had to let the leadership of the organization in on his vision, and second—and most important—he had to start acting like a leader *right now!*

Not all of my clients take my advice, but he did. In less than three months, he became the organization's general sales manager.

It amazes me how many people believe that once they get the position, they will *then* assume its responsibilities. But the importance of getting a vision and believing in it is that it causes you to act like it's true *right now*. Who do you think management is looking for? People waiting to be discovered, or people who are behaving like leaders *right now?* Leaders don't choose complainers and fault-finders to be new leaders. They select people who already have the right attitude and demonstrate it daily.

Have a vision of yourself as a great leader. Don't get hung up on *how* you should act. Instead, think about and find out *what* the best outcome would be for others. Remember, have a vision, and the "how" will follow.

When should you begin acting like a good leader? *Right now.* Not tomorrow, not next week, and not after you take a leadership class. Act like a leader now.

Great leaders orchestrate others to create and articulate the vision and then ask, "How are we going to get this done?" They don't dictate how things should be done. If a leader or manager tells employees how something is going to be done, there's no buy-in. In order to get buy-in, you must solicit employee input and really listen to what they have to say. *Then* the creative juices will begin to flow; *and* synergies create the outcome.

Imagine working for a leader who is interested in your success. Even though the organization has specific things it must accomplish, this leader is still looking out for your well-being and seeks your feedback, too, asking questions like, "How do *you* think we can tackle this? What do *you* think we ought to do?" How exciting would working for that person be, versus working for a boss who only tells you what to do? There's a huge difference. Remember, it's the difference that makes the difference.

Other Important Points for Leaders

Another key element of leadership is treating everyone, no matter what their position, equally. People notice quickly if you have "favorites" or otherwise treat people differently. No one wants to feel left out.

As much as possible, leaders should avoid seeking recognition for something a team, department, or other group is involved with. This means giving up the need to receive credit for successes. It can be difficult, because we're conditioned to believe that the person who gets the credit wins. That's simply not true. The best leaders don't need outside recognition to build their self-esteem; they know in their hearts what they've done and what they've achieved. That's how leaders build self-esteem—from the inside out, rather than the outside in.

Of course, you must recognize your successes within yourself. Celebrate, yell, and do whatever you need to do to recognize your victories—but always do it on your own time and in your own mind. You, too, will "meet with a success unexpected in common hours."

What We're All Selling

Being a great leader means having to do many things, including selling. This shouldn't come as a surprise. We are all in the sales business. We are all selling something—our ideas, our products, and even our vision. The old axiom is true: People hate to be sold, but love to buy. As a leader, never sell anything to your people if you want buy-in. Get them excited, seek their input, and find out how they believe they will profit from reaching the organizational vision. Then you won't have to sell them on it—they'll be thrilled to buy on their own terms.

A Final Note

Work is supposed to be *inspiring*, not *perspiring*. Leaders are a key factor in differentiating between the two. Great leaders build up their people, knowing that the resulting synergies will cause an organization to soar to even greater heights. These leaders must deflect personal recognition away from themselves and turn it toward others. This is always difficult, because people would rather be *right* than be successful and most want recognition from others.

But true leaders rely on their internal beliefs and values to achieve prosperity. They don't rely on others for recognition. When a leader builds up others, recognition comes, no matter what. I'd rather have no recognition at all for helping someone succeed than be recognized for holding them back. How about you? The greatest leaders of all are servant leaders, creating environments for others to succeed.

Epilogue

A s you may picked up from the reading of this book, I've got a few years under my belt. Some would say that I have reached an age where I have gained the wisdom of experience. Indeed, I've had many experiences, and thankfully a certain degree of knowledge has been a positive result of them. One thing I've learned, without question, is that the information in this book can be hugely powerful in transforming lives, families, and organizations. However, it is of no value at all if it's not put into practice. I'd like to share with you one of my life experiences that illustrates the power of application and explains best as to why this book exists.

Many years ago, I landed a job as director of operations for a franchise organization. The application of concepts in this book had taken the organization to new heights. I was responsible for a team of five general managers. I was successful and made good money. Heck, I was even driving a Jaguar. I had recently divorced after 12 years of marriage and moved to a new neighborhood to be close to my children. I was seven months into a new position, new surroundings, and nice wheels—I was well on my way to a whole new life.

One day, the company's owner returned from Europe to tell me my services were no longer required. I had until 3 p.m. to clean out my office and say goodbye to my team. The usual emotional responses ensued: shock, confusion, denial, and anger. Once beyond the tears and outrage, I realized that I had a problem. A really big problem. I had no severance check, no job, and many financial responsibilities. I was very qualified and experienced, so was it really such a big deal? All I needed was a new *vision*, but I'd built a scotoma to that. I was focused on the *problem* instead.

I went job hunting, but after six months, I was still a free agent. I'd had several interviews and had even been offered a couple of jobs, but they wouldn't cover child support and my other obligations. I needed something more, something better.

One my best options was a speakers bureau to whom I'd sent a video and promotional material about some concepts I'd been studying and applying throughout my career. Even though it didn't pay as well as the job I just lost, it seemed a decent plan, given my dwindling savings at that time. Finally, a response arrived. "At last, a break," I thought, tearing the envelope open. You can imagine my pain as I read the rejection letter—another huge ROX in my bucket.

With nothing else on the horizon, I began to get very nervous. I had exhausted my savings and didn't know how I was going to pay my bills. I was totally focused on the fact that I didn't have a job. It was a vicious circle of problem-panic-problem. I knew something drastic had to happen, but I was incapable of proactive, constructive thought because I was so lost in my dilemma. Life was bleak. I was depressed. My self-esteem was at an all-time low. All I could think about was how bad things were, and how everyone else was so much better off. My current reality was far from prosperous.

By necessity, I trimmed all the "fat," sold the Jaguar, and arranged to share an old Mazda pickup with my daughter, Gretchen, who was living with me while she attended high school. She was amazingly supportive, but a teen still has street credibility to protect. (She wouldn't have friends over for fear that they might see Morose Out-of-Work Father sporting a worn-out bathrobe.) When you're depressed, your Rox-Talk is all about how bad your situation is and how worthless you are. Despite my family's support and love, I was feeling pretty sorry for myself at this time.

Remember, I already *knew* all the information I've just shared with you in this book. I had studied and educated others about how incredible we are for over 30 years and created many new programs. I knew that whatever a man can conceive, he can achieve. I became a living testament to it. I had conceived of joblessness, poverty, and worthlessness and as a result, I was experiencing it. I had never been in a situation where I had allowed the circumstances I was in to take over my life.

Having resigned myself to failure and desperation, I created that reality. No matter how smart and together I thought I sounded to interviewers, I unconsciously sent over hundreds of thousands of messages like, "I probably won't get this job because..." or "It doesn't matter anyway; I don't like this line of work." At the time, I had a scotoma to the messages I was sending, and a scotoma to *the possibility of changing my reality.*

At the edge of reason and financial ruin, however, came a turning point. I had just turned 47. I was still telling myself how rotten life was, and what a failure I had become to my family and friends. Suddenly, I had an epiphany. I finally realized that in my current mental condition, particularly at my advancing age, I'd *never* get a job! I had been preaching for years that vision creates reality. That was it. How could I have forgotten such a critical reality? It's simple: I didn't know what I was thinking, because I only paid attention to what I was experiencing.

Suddenly, I understood that my attitude and approach were totally unacceptable. All the knowledge I had gained, practiced, and taught over the years came flooding back, smashing through the debilitating scotomas my depression had built. I knew that I could change things. Like Dorothy and her ruby slippers, I'd always had the power to "go home." I'd just wandered from my path and gotten lost in the obstacles. Now I knew that if I could envision my future, I could reach it. I could get home again.

I remembered that a former colleague had once told me, "The best way to get a job is to hire yourself, and to do that, you need to be in business for yourself." In those liberating post-epiphany moments (knowing that I had to do *something* different), I considered the possibility. Reflexively, my next thought was, "I don't know how. I've never done that before." I didn't have a clue about what to do or how to begin. I took a moment, and remembered, "Hold on. The *how* will come, I just need the vision." I held onto the vision of starting my own company like a life raft in the ocean, knowing that if I let go, I would surely drown. If you get a vision and live it, hang on, because the abundant and joyful life you are supposed to live will lift you out of poverty and sorrow.

My ember of a vision was about to explode into a blazing inferno. The phone rang. Expecting another bill collector, I answered the phone cautiously. The caller was Kevin Whalen, the general manager of Sterling McCall Toyota in Houston, Texas.

"A friend of mine," he said, "told me that you had your own company and that I should give you a call."

I was either dreaming or my vision was on steroids. I looked around the room at the cluttered remains of a half-year of uncertainty and forced economy. "Yes," I answered, "I have my own company. What can I do for you?" My RAS dialed in, and I was back on the path to changing my reality.

Kevin explained that he had heard that I'd played an instrumental part in the success of his friend's training program. He said, "I don't really know *why* we might need you. We already have a great team, and we are currently the number eight Toyota dealership in the country."

I thought for a moment and said, "Just a hunch, but when you were little and picking teams for a game, were you the captain?"

"Yes."

I asked him another question. "Today, now that you are the captain of your dealership, you feel pretty good about your team, don't you?"

Once more he replied in the affirmative, so I continued, "OK, but how about the people who were picked last for teams when they were growing up? How do you think they feel?"

There was a long pause before he said, "Larry, how do I get you to come out here?" It was a clear indication of his abilities as a leader. He knew that how his people felt about themselves was critical to their success in life, and the more success they experienced, the more his company benefited. We agreed on the terms and a time to meet in Houston for the next week. Just like that I was back.

I put down the phone and fell into the nearest chair. I had only just decided to start my own business when I got a phone call requesting my services! Coincidence, you may think, but I don't believe in coincidences. Relieved and more than a little amazed, I realized I had a world of excitement ahead. I'd arranged an appointment for which I needed to be totally prepared. Rather than worrying about the next interview I couldn't have been more pumped. My company was taking on a new structure. Armed with the new vision I had only three days until I was expected in Houston. Bring it on!

Remember the power of vision—it forces us to look *forward*. Remember how you feel when you are looking forward? You become motivated. You do whatever is necessary to pull off whatever it is you are looking forward to doing, achieving, and obtaining. Until that phone rang, I had been looking *backward* at all the things I had done, and what others had done to me. I had created my own reality, my own depression, and my own inability to get hired or achieve anything else I wanted. I'd forgotten how blessed we all are. But now it was time to *transform* myself—just making a few changes wouldn't be enough. It was time to *burn the bathrobe!*

I began in earnest to formulate and implement my plans, and my company started to take shape. Constantly reinforcing my vision, I scratched out a rough business plan and printed business cards. My ticket arrived. I dusted off my best suit and shoes and arrived in Houston a few days later. On the plane, I realized that I had another challenge in that my program didn't have a formal name. It was time to let the miraculous brain do its job. Since my education and studies had focused on how thinking is essential to success, I thought the name should reflect that phenomenon. And as excellence is not too grand a term to describe human potential, the name *Lessons In the Fundamentals of Excellence* was adopted, with the acronym of L.I.F.E.

I spent a sleepless night before the presentation. When it was time to meet Kevin Whalen at last, I took a deep breath and entered his office. He shook my hand warmly and made me feel like I'd just made a great friend. He asked me to explain my program. Excitedly, I told him that I could teach people that performance is dictated by thinking, and that when they learn how to change their thinking, performance follows. It was really all about teaching people how to create a new perspective.

I asked him if he was interested in improving his organization's performance; he was, but he told me that I'd have to sell the boss over lunch. An hour later over lunch at an exclusive country club, I met another remarkable and generous man—Sterling McCall himself.

At that point, there were only a few degrees of separation between me and my bathrobe, but I was holding an ace. I had a vision, and I knew how I wanted it to play out. They wanted to hear all about the program—how long it was, if there were companion materials, how much it was, and how long a commitment they'd need to make. When I told them the cost I held my breath through what seemed an endless pause in the conversation, and they eventually agreed to buy three packages: one for each store.

Back home, I bought a computer, pulled out all the programs I had created throughout the years, for the next five days, from seven in the morning until eleven at night, I wrote the first L.I.F.E. manual. Bound copies in hand, I returned to Houston to conduct my first program. Standing in front of 30 judges —a group of executives who had seen it all—was a "perform or die" moment. I have to say that it was the *first* L.I.F.E. program I had ever given, and undoubtedly the *worst*. After the first lesson, McCall told me, "Larry, don't bother trying to sell your program to my other two stores."

I took an emotional step backwards, teetering at the edge of the black abyss. I was nearly convinced of my old belief, abject failure, when he added, "You needn't bother [selling it], because this program is so powerful, you're already in." He shook my hand to seal the deal. To this day, I still become emotional when I recall that moment.

That one phone call led to a one-year contract that continued for seven years. Within the first two years after implementing Aperneo's programs, the McCall organization climbed to second in the country for their Toyota store and sixth in the country for their Lexus store. The organization's profits doubled, and it reached their five-year vision in three. Kevin Whalen became the platform president for the McCall group. Since then, Kevin has moved on to start several of his own companies. He continues to expand his organization and attain the results he and his associates seek by making his people his number one priority. I'm truly blessed to still be a part of his incredible success. It is an endless joy to see the success of my other clients as well. They also realize that you make your organization great when you've created a culture that encourages and nurtures its people to be the best that they can be.

McCall was the first of many new accounts, and since that time, my company has reached a level of success far beyond my hopes and expectations. Twenty two years later, Aperneo, LLC and its programs continue to provide meaningful education to organizations and individuals. I'm currently leading the creation and development of the Haselwood University who's purpose is Creating Remarkable Experiences for Each Other and our Communities with Integrity, Respect and Loyalty. From bathrobe to dean of a university. Who would of thunk? What's your vision? It's certainly possible if you'll just envision.

In Closing

The story of how my company came into existence, and flourished, is proof of the effectiveness of this message. I was so locked-on to a defeatist mentality that I had built a scotoma to my own obstructive behavior. I couldn't move ahead—in fact, I couldn't move at all—because my Rox-Talk was supporting my then-current reality, keeping me firmly entrenched in it. All I could *see* was that which matched my thinking.

Fortunately, the power of vision is limitless. It becomes the catalyst that makes available to us everything we need to manifest our hopes and dreams. Back in my "bathrobe days," all the principles of the L.I.F.E. lessons taught in this book were fully in play. I was getting everything that matched my vision; my problem was that I had the wrong vision.

What's your vision? Stop and listen to how you talk to yourself, and it will appear. Is it what you want? If not, change your vision, and your performance will follow; it has no other choice.

We may not have met yet, but we actually know each other very well. In fact, we're very similar. To you, I may be a head shot on a book cover, and my words are little more than black ink on a white page. But just as yours does, my life goes precisely where I allow it to go. Your incredible brain functions in the same way as mine. We all have the ability to get exactly what we need, and what we want. We never know when this may be our last moment in this thing called L.I.F.E., but if this is mine, I can honestly say I left this world "having the time of my life *right now*."

Where are you headed on this phenomenal journey? Can you see prosperity in your future and live as if you have it now? Do you have all that you need to live a truly inspiring life? Trust me, God has blessed us with more than enough. But if you're not taking action on what you've learned, then you're currently living a shadow of what your life is truly meant to be.

Life is for living *now*, my friend. It's time to come out and play, today and every day hereafter. You get to decide what you will play and how you're feeling while you're playing it. You just need to believe first, and let the evidence appear.

You will live the life you've envisioned. The power of vision is truly amazing, no matter what your current circumstances are. Draw the line and take your stand. *Get a vision and live it* so you can truly be the best for the world.

God bless,

Larry Olsen
Founder and CEO, Aperneo LLC
Washington State

About the Author *Larry Olsen*

Author • Speaker • Educator • Corporate Success Coach

Larry Olsen's success attitude is contagious. Corporations large and small partner up with Olsen to design and implement practical, results-producing applications of his programs for individuals and as well as groups. His expertise is based in part on a wealth of hands-on achievements as an award-winning educator, as the successful gen-eral manager of a large, multi-franchise company, head of a University and as the Founder of Aperneo LLC, a 21st Century Success Consultancy since 1995.

Olsen knows that corporate success hinges on the attitudes and actions of individuals: If an organization is to be successful, its people must come first—no shortcuts, and no excuses. With proper training, people can and will learn to perform at peak levels while supporting their teams' larger visions. Everyone Larry works with gains the personal strength and insight to conquer their fears and failures, and the motivation to carry life-renewing confidence into their everyday lives while accomplishing their loftiest visions. As Larry says, "Leadership must look at the big picture while at the same time realizing that overall performance is merely an indication of how successful each individual is."

Larry Olsen's inspiring and visionary work in human success and achievement is rooted in his own life story. His value-oriented, sky-is-the-limit outlook is the right pre-scription for dynamic business and personal success, and demonstrates the ease with which we can all manifest our visions. Larry lives with his wife and best friend, Diane, and their children in the great Washington State.

See the website at **www.aperneo.com** and contact Larry at **success@aperneo.com.**

About Aperneo, LLC

Aperneo's cognitive approach to achieving excellence is as unique as it is effective. Six powerful programs form the basis of Aperneo's systems.

Lessons in the Fundamentals of Excellence (L.I.F.E.^{sm})

Focuses on how the brain functions, learns, and handles changes. It shows people how they acquired their current beliefs and how they can change attitudes that block success, keeping them from having the time of their lives right now!

Vision Building

Creates the synergies companies are looking for. If you're putting together a jigsaw puzzle without a box top to look at, how do you know what you're working toward? This exciting program unleashes your most valuable asset—your people—to create a vision so powerful that performance soars, and old records crumble.

Coaching Excellence in Others (C.E.O.^{sm})

Trains managers and selected leaders as coaches, showing them how to draw out the powerful and compelling visions of their team members and identify their own perceptions of their challenges. Armed with this knowledge, they can attach agreed upon time-lines to their ultimate solutions. The end result is vision fulfillment, which maximizes their individual performance and accelerates their team's performance as well.

Executive Coaching

All about creating a new perspective. Looking at the same issues day in and day out requires a fresh perspective if accelerated growth is to occur. This one-on-one time takes into account the "lonely-at-the-top" factor, and provides leaders with some company. The program provides opportunities and strategies to align current behaviors with personal, as well as organizational, visions.

LEADERSHIP

A 10-segment program, based on the fact that organizational performance is either limited or accelerated by current leadership. Leadership should inspire and grow its people. Each segment uncovers the essential elements necessary for leading people beyond what's currently thought possible.

Actualizing Futures Through Efficacious Rehearsal (AFTER Life[sm])

Designed for L.I.F.E. graduates who are thirsty for more. AFTER Life begins where L.I.F.E. left off and fuses the key concepts into finely crafted, easy to use tools that are essential for those who want to overcome challenges and reach vision.

For more information:

success@aperneo.com

www.aperneo.com

218

Quick Order Form

WEB | www.aperneo.com

CONTACT | success@aperneo.com

Please send me _____ copies of **Get a Vision and Live It!**
at $24.95 each, plus shipping and handling.
(Save! If you order 10 copies or more, the price is only $19.95 each.)

Please send me _____ copies of **LIFE, The Audio Program** on CD
at $49.95 plus shipping and handling.

Name_____Date_____

Address_____

City_____State_____Zip_____

Phone_____Email_____

Sales Tax: Please add 9%.
Shipping in the US: $6 for the first book/audio program and $2 for each additional book/
audio program. **International Shipping:** Based on ship-to location and current rates;
please call for exact amounts.

Payment Type: _____Check/Money order enclosed _____Visa _____MC _____Amex

Credit Card #_____

Name on Card_____Exp. Date_____

Signature_____

Phone Number_____

Quick Order Form

WEB | www.aperneo.com

CONTACT | success@aperneo.com

Please send me _____ copies of **Get a Vision and Live It!**
at $24.95 each, plus shipping and handling.
(Save! If you order 10 copies or more, the price is only $19.95 each.)

Please send me _____ copies of **LIFE, The Audio Program** on CD
at $49.95 plus shipping and handling.

Name_____Date_____

Address_____

City_____State_____Zip_____

Phone_____Email_____

Sales Tax: Please add 9%.
Shipping in the US: $6 for the first book/audio program and $2 for each additional book/ audio program. **International Shipping:** Based on ship-to location and current rates; please call for exact amounts.

Payment Type: _____Check/Money order enclosed _____Visa _____MC _____Amex

Credit Card #_____

Name on Card_____Exp. Date_____

Signature_____

Phone Number_____